MOON METRO
CHICAGO

AVALON
TRAVEL

TABLE OF CONTENTS

CITY MAPS

CITY LIFE

INTRODUCTION TO CHICAGO

Upon arriving in Chicago, the first thing you notice is its famous skyline, the collection of iconic buildings that declare the city to be the Midwest's towering center of culture and commerce. Like all bustling metropolises, Chicago spills out over several hundred square miles, incorporating dozens of neighborhoods and several suburbs.

Few big cities get an opportunity to start over from scratch, but in Chicago's case the rare mandate came as a mixed blessing. Whether or not you believe the story of Mrs. O'Leary's anxious cow, there's no question that the Great Fire of 1871 was devastating. Reducing huge swathes of the city to ashes and rubble, the fire put a halt to much of Chicago's phenomenal progress, which had shot a steady upward arc since the first pelt traders settled the area back in 1779.

However, the disaster served to show Chicago's strength. Within 20 years, the city was ready to host the world during the 1893 Columbian Exposition. In advance of the international gathering, Chicago had embarked on a massive building boom that created several city icons, from the Art Institute to the elevated train system (the El). Just as significant was the city's new development plan: a grid system, courtesy of Daniel Burnham, to better serve and connect the still-burgeoning population. With dozens of other architects and designers commissioned, Chicago had gone to work and the result was a true 20th-century urban center.

During the redevelopment of its identity, Chicago earned a reputation as a tough town thanks to larger-than-life figures like Al Capone and the first Mayor Richard Daley. The days of powerful gangsters and political riots are long gone, particularly since the city began its late '70s comeback, but

Chicago still exudes a certain stubborn, straightforward charm. At the very least, Chicago residents need a thick skin to survive the brutal winters, when frigid gusts whip across Lake Michigan to create brag-worthy wind chills. Chicago's "Windy City" nickname originally referred to the blowhard local politicians, but its dual application is undeniable. But even the coldest days of a dwindling winter promise the imminent arrival of another beautiful Chicago spring. In fact, once warm weather finally hits and the city thaws, Chicago blooms into action. Frolickers pack the beaches and families return to the parks.

The many such outdoor areas make up a large part of the city's character, as Chicagoans value open space as a welcome contrast to the huge skyscrapers. The broad boulevards and botanical traffic islands break up all the imposing buildings, but the ambitious heights of the Sears Tower and John Hancock Center are almost never out of view. The dense downtown epicenter draws attention away from the city's impressive sprawl, the reaches of which are the destination of all those people clogging the highways at rush hour.

Indeed, this sprawl is ironically one of Chicago's greatest attributes. Unlike other urban centers, Chicago gives you breathing room as well as an endless supply of things to do. You can drive to the outer points of the city, or spend your entire time within walking distance of the Loop and feel equally fulfilled. Visitors should think big but start small, easing their way into this cosmopolitan, cultural Mecca of the Midwest.

UNFOLD THE PAGE FOR

- OVERVIEW MAP
- HOW TO USE THIS BOOK

CITY LIFE

TOP SPOTS

We've profiled the best of the city, including top sights, restaurants, shops, amusements, and hotels. To find any listing's location, turn to the neighborhood map in the front of the book and find its grid coordinates.

CHARLIE TROTTER'S

A conservative, moneyed clientele comes for the top-notch service and superlative cuisine at this world-famous restaurant. Book months in advance and leave yourself lots of time to work through the fixed-price meals, a melange of American, French, and Asian influences. $$$ ———— Price key

Neighborhood map ———— locator

B1 816 W. ARMITAGE AVE.
773-248-6228

Map grid coordinates

PRICE KEY

RESTAURANTS:

$	Entrées under $10
$$	Entrées $10–20
$$$	Entrées over $20

HOTELS:

$	Rooms under $200
$$	Rooms $200–300
$$$	Rooms over $300

SIDE WALKS

SIDE
WALKS

With some major sights you'll find a list of things to do nearby.

· Stroll Alta Vista Terrace
A2 START AT N. ALTA VISTA TER. AND GRACE ST.

· Trove Flashy Trash for vintage costumes.
B3 3524 N. HALSTED ST. 773-327-6900

· Ann Sather for pre-game Swedish meatballs
C3 929 W. BELMONT AVE. 773-348-2378

· Raise a glass for the team at Murphy's Bleachers
B3 3655 N. SHEFFIELD AVE. 773-281-5356

STREET INDEX

A comprehensive street index is located at the back of the book.

Map reference

HOW TO USE THIS BOOK

CITY MAPS

NEIGHBORHOODS

We've divided the city into nine distinct, but overlapping, neighborhoods. For easy identification, each has been assigned a color, used on the map itself and in easy-to-spot icons throughout the listings.

1 LOOP EAST / GRANT PARK / MUSEUM CAMPUS

2 WEST LOOP

3 MAGNIFICENT MILE

4 RIVER NORTH / RIVER WEST

5 GOLD COAST / OLD TOWN / LINCOLN PARK SOUTH

6 BUCKTOWN / WICKER PARK

7 LAKE VIEW / LINCOLN PARK NORTH

8 SOUTH LOOP / BURNHAM PARK

9 HYDE PARK

GUIDES TO THE MAPS

Next to each map is a grid-by-grid guide to the very best sights, restaurants, shops, amusements, and hotels in the neighborhood.

Map grid coordinates ———
Ⓡ **RESTAURANTS** pp. 29-42

B1
- CAFE BA-BA-REEBA!, p. 32
- CHARLIE TROTTER'S, p. 33 ——— Find a complete description on this page.

Street nam

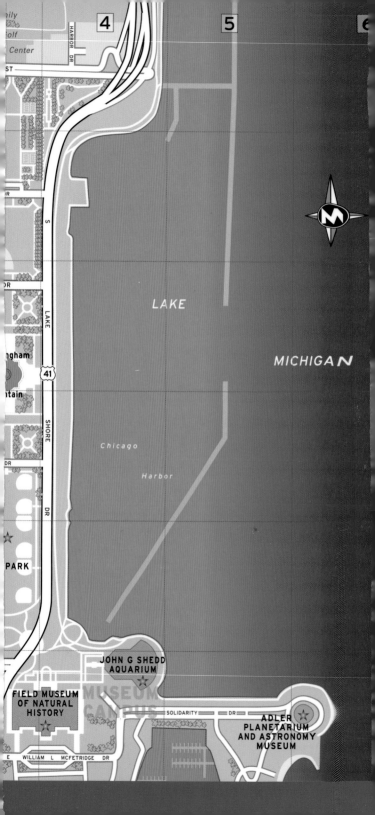

ily
olf
Center
ST

HARBOR DR

S

R

DR

LAKE

ngham

41

ntain

SHORE

DR

DR

PARK

LAKE

MICHIGAN

Chicago

Harbor

JOHN G SHEDD
AQUARIUM

FIELD MUSEUM
OF NATURAL
HISTORY

MUSEUM
CAMPUS

SOLIDARITY DR

ADLER
PLANETARIUM
AND ASTRONOMY
MUSEUM

E

WILLIAM L MCFETRIDGE DR

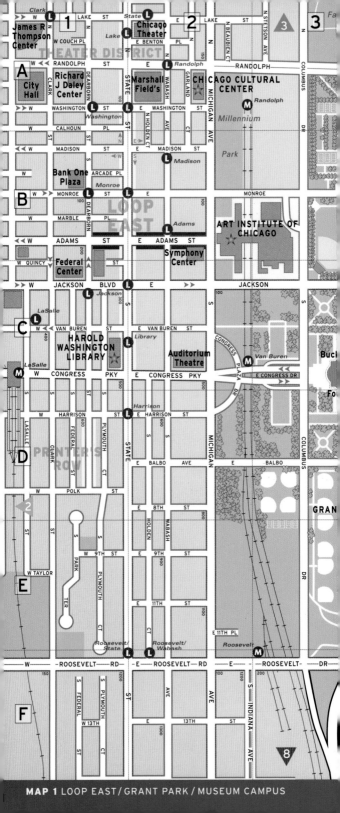

MAP 1 LOOP EAST / GRANT PARK / MUSEUM CAMPUS

LOOP EAST / GRANT PARK / MUSEUM CAMPUS

 The lakeshore east of the Loop boasts a concentration of world-class museums and must-see sights, offers gorgeous views, and even contains the city's "front yard." In other words, this area is Chicago's welcome to the world.

Visitors to Loop East should have no trouble finding their way around Chicago's predictable grid-system streets. If you need some help, though, the neoclassic Cultural Center, home of the Office of Tourism's Visitor Information Center, is a natural first stop.

Dominating the waterfront is Grant Park and its expanse of green and flowers. This warm-weather haven is the site of several festivals, free concerts from Chicago Symphony Orchestra, and the Taste of Chicago, a flurry of food and fireworks that peaks around the Fourth of July. Also in the park is Buckingham Fountain, one of the city's most recognizable landmarks, spraying water over passing motorists whenever the breeze shifts.

At the northwestern corner of the park, you'll find the Art Institute, which showcases of one of the world's greatest collections of paintings, sculptures, and arcana from the Middle Ages right up to the present. Sitting right across the street, Symphony Center hosts indoor renditions of CSO concerts. With the restaurants along Adams Street and the nearby Auditorium Theatre and its resident Joffrey Ballet, this part of the Loop draws cabloads of well-dressed arts patrons once the seasons start.

This far south, Michigan Avenue and its surrounding streets don't display the same level of consumer exuberance as the Magnificent Mile, but thanks to a number of prominent hotels, schools, and the occasional museum, the area

MAP 1 LOOP EAST / GRANT PARK / MUSEUM CAMPUS

MAP 1

remains crowded with cars nonetheless. To sate that shopping desire, walk a few blocks west to State Street, where
the grand Marshall Field's flagship stands as a Chicago institution, and the stretch between the river and Congress
Parkway is dotted with stores.

Heading further south, toward the end of Grant Park,
Chicago's famed Museum Campus combines three of the
city's most popular attractions: the Shedd Aquarium, Field
Museum, and Adler Planetarium. The aquarium and planetarium sit right alongside the lake, while the Field Museum is
set only slightly inland, looming next to crowded Lake Shore
Drive. No visit to Chicago is complete without spending a
few hours at any of these sights – just be sure to arrive
early whenever there's a football game or a convention
since Bears fans and conventioneers headed to Soldier Field
and McCormick Place, nearby in the South Loop, can clog
the area with traffic.

Often matching Lake Shore Drive in terms of gridlock is the
immensely popular path that runs along Lake Michigan.
Bikers, joggers, walkers, and in-line skaters vie for space
along the two-lane strip, while drivers slow down to gawk at
all the action on the beach. But by the time the weather
picks up no one seems to be in a hurry anyway, so the con-
gestion often comes as a leisurely change of pace from the
usual rush of metropolitan motorists.

1 UNFOLD FOR MAP

LOOP EAST / GRANT PARK / MUSEUM CA

★ SIGHTS pp. 1-28

A2
· CHICAGO CULTURAL CENTER, p. 7

B2
· ART INSTITUTE OF CHICAGO, p. 4

C1
· HAROLD WASHINGTON
  LIBRARY, p. 14

E3
· GRANT PARK, p. 13

F4
· FIELD MUSEUM OF NATURAL
  HISTORY, p. 11
· JOHN G. SHEDD AQUARIUM, p. 15

F6
· ADLER PLANETARIUM AND
  ASTRONOMY MUSEUM, p. 2

® RESTAURANTS pp. 29-42

A2
· WALNUT ROOM, p. 42

B1
· ITALIAN VILLAGE, p. 35

B2
· RHAPSODY, p. 39
· RUSSIAN TEA TIME, p. 40

C2
· ZOOM KITCHEN, p. 42

ⓢ SHOPS pp. 43-54

A2
· MARSHALL FIELD'S, p. 51

B2
· CARSON PIRIE SCOTT & CO., p. 47
· FANNIE MAY CANDIES, p. 48
· WABASH JEWELERS MALL, p. 54

C1
· GARRETT POPCORN SHOPS, p. 49

C2
· AFROCENTRIC BOOKSTORE, p. 46
· CROW'S NEST RECORDS, p. 47
· PRAIRIE AVENUE BOOKSHOP, p. 52
· THE SAVVY TRAVELLER, p. 52

MAP LEGEND

★ SIGHTS
ⓛ EL STOP
Ⓜ METRA STOP
▽5 ADJACENT MAP

DAYTIME HOT SPOTS
NIGHTTIME HOT SPOTS
DAY AND NIGHT
CLOSED TO TRAFFIC

Approximate distance across map: 1.5 mi

0   0.25 mile

0   0.25 kilometer

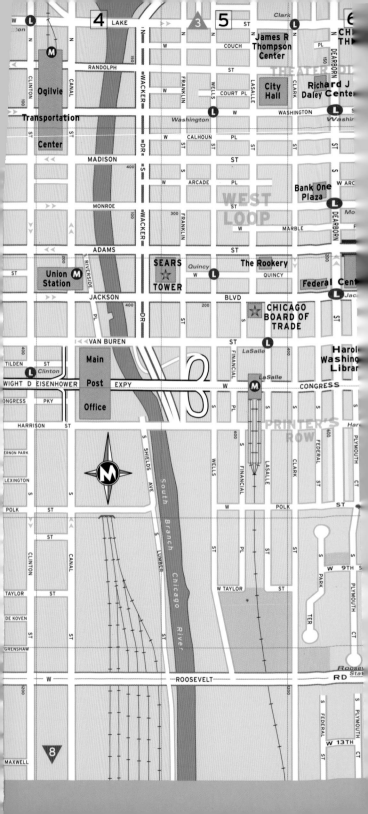

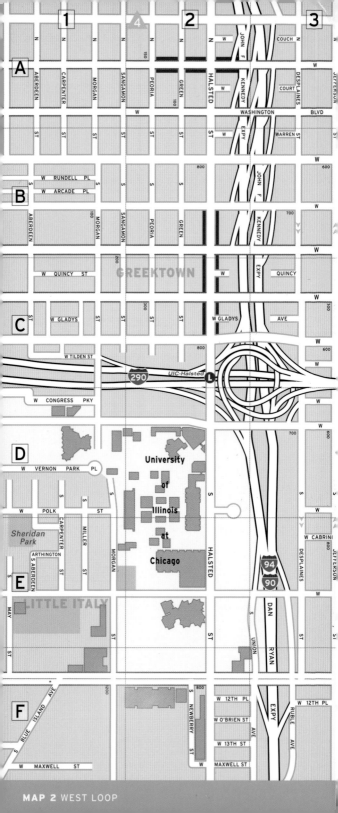

MAP 2 WEST LOOP

MAP 2

WEST LOOP

The skyscraper- and public art-spotted arteries of the West Loop accommodate many of the symbols that put Chicago on the map. The financial and theater districts, warehouses, and architectural icons all are situated around the elevated tracks that give this area its name.

The West Loop's most prominent sight also happens to be the city's key building mascot, the Sears Tower. For architecture buffs who come to see the tallest building in the United States, there are numerous other treats lying in its long shadow, from the art deco Board of Trade to the futuristic James R. Thompson Center.

The warehouses and industrial zones that once defined the area right outside downtown have now been converted to condos and luxury lofts, making this a neighborhood of people as well as buildings. Forget about affordable housing, though – the West Loop has grown so crowded that even parking spots are often bartered and sold for exorbitant prices.

South of downtown on Dearborn is Printer's Row, a classy clatch of big lofts and restaurants that exude old Chicago character – meaning vegetarians should call ahead to confirm menu options. A nod to its previous claim to fame as the center of Chicago's printing industry, Printer's Row features an annual book fair that pulls in many of the Midwest's most prominent new and used sellers.

The West Loop is also where multimedia mogul and celebrity Oprah Winfrey records her daily show each morning. While Harpo Studios is easy to find, tickets, on the other hand, can be hard to come by on short notice. Plan ahead or talk to a well-connected concierge, and you could get lucky.

UNFOLD FOR MAP

MAP 2 WEST LOOP

WEST LOOP

MAP LEGEND

★	SIGHTS		DAYTIME HOT SPOTS
Ⓛ	EL STOP		NIGHTTIME HOT SPOTS
Ⓜ	METRA STOP		DAY AND NIGHT
▽5	ADJACENT MAP		CLOSED TO TRAFFIC

Approximate distance across map: 1.6 mi

0   0.25 mile

0   0.25 kilometer

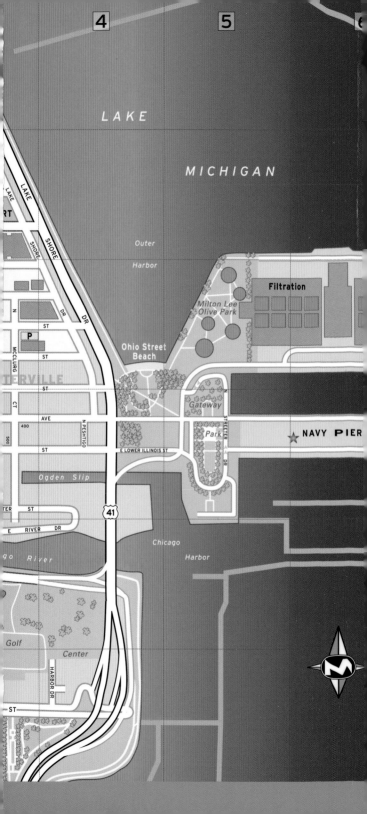

4 **5** 6

LAKE

MICHIGAN

Outer

Harbor

Filtration

Milton Lee
Olive Park

Ohio Street
Beach

LAKE SHORE DR

LAKE SHORE DR

N ST

N ST

N ST

P

McCLURG

ST

CT

AVE

400

N PESHTIGO

500

ST

Gateway

Park

N STREETER DR

★ NAVY PIER

E LOWER ILLINOIS ST

Ogden Slip

ER ST

41

E RIVER DR

go River

Chicago

Harbor

Golf

Center

HARBOR DR

ST

TERVILLE

W MAPLE ST **1** GOLD COAST **2** **5** **3**

E BELLEVUE PL

A W OAK ST | E OAK ST | E LAKE SHORE DR

W WALTON ST | WALTON | PL

900 N Michigan

W DELAWARE | DELAWARE | PL

JOHN HANCOCK CENTER ★

CHESTNUT

W CHESTNUT ST | **Water Tower Place**

B PEARSON

WATER TOWER ★ | **MUSEUM OF CONTEMPORARY**

W CHICAGO AVE Ⓛ | CHICAGO | 100 ★ | AVE

Chicago

W SUPERIOR ST | E SUPERIOR | ST | **Northwester**

W HURON ST | E HURON | ST | **University**

MAGNIFICENT MILE

C W ERIE ST | E | ERIE

W ONTARIO ST | **P**

600 N Michigan | ONTARIO

W OHIO ST | OHIO | **STRE**

D W GRAND AVE Ⓛ | Grand | GRAND

W ILLINOIS ST | ILLINOIS

W HUBBARD ST | HUBBARD | **Tribune Tower**

W KINZIE ST | KINZIE | **Wrigley Building** | NORTH

Marina City | **MICHIGAN AVENUE BRIDGE** ★

E WACKER | Chic

W WACKER DR | E WACKER PL | E SOUTH WATER ST

Family

E HADDOCK PL | State

W LAKE ST Ⓛ | LAKE | ST | RANDOLPH

Chicago Theater Ⓛ | E BENTON PL

THEATER DISTRICT

W RANDOLPH ST Ⓛ | Randolph

F **Marshall Field's** | **Chicago Cultural Center** | Millennium Park

Ⓛ WASHINGTON Ⓛ | E WASHINGTON | Ⓜ Randolph

MAP 3 MAGNIFICENT MILE

MAGNIFICENT MILE

Vertical malls, expensive hotels, sidewalk flower patches, and boutique shops line this tract of Michigan Avenue and conspicuous consumers crowd its manicured walkways. A manageable (if usually congested) walk, Magnificent Mile proper stretches from the Chicago River to Oak Street, but trying to cover the entire distance in one go may not be the best strategy. In fact, shopping pros have learned to split the distance into two separate trips so that by the end of the Mile, they aren't loaded down with bags.

Chicago's novel method of making space for all the stores is, instead of building out, the city builds *up*. The best example of these multilevel structures may be Water Tower Place (not to be confused with the actual Water Tower, a nearby survivor from before the Great Fire). Incorporating the five-star Ritz-Carlton hotel, Water Tower Place also holds a spa, two department stores, and popular shops. The bottom floor is taken up by Food Life, a sprawling court of quick bites popular with business lunchers and shopaholics needing to fuel up. Right around the corner is the Museum of Contemporary Art, in austere contrast to the busy buying-and-selling spots.

Sometimes the sidewalks themselves provide plenty of distractions. Recent years have seen them decorated by fiberglass cows and weatherproof couches, and the city keeps hundreds of bright flowers blooming. If you see people lined up, that could mean you're coming up on one of the famous Garrett Popcorn Shops, which draw scores of people with irresistible caramel and cheese corn. Just be sure to wipe off your hands before walking through the Fort Knox–like

MAP 3 MAGNIFICENT MILE

MAP 3

doors of Tiffany's – sticky sugar and orange cheese dust tend to devalue the diamonds.

Besides the consumerist fervor surrounding the area, landmark buildings make this mile magnificent. Just over the Chicago River is the Wrigley Building, a bright white slab that's lit up by spotlights at night. Nearby is the *Chicago Tribune* Tower, the walls of which are inlaid with bricks from dozens of famous international sites. Its prime competitor, the *Chicago Sun-Times,* is located almost right across the street on Wabash, but the bland building itself is so underwheming that a redesign is finally in the works. The baroquely ornate Hotel Inter-Continental makes a romantic stay at the foot of the Mile. Farther north, the historic Water Tower has stood in its place since 1869 and the 100-floor John Hancock Center tops them all.

Not to be outdone, Navy Pier, the spit of landfill jutting out into the lake, is packed almost year-round thanks to the all-in-one selection of museums, tours, stores, and restaurants. Scorned by locals, the former navy training ground is unabashedly touristy, and offers a combination of unique attractions, like a museum of stained glass, and once-is-enough activities.

Not shopped out? Try Oak Street for its concentration of boutiques between Michigan and Rush. And for those with energy to spare, Rush Street, cutting diagonally northwest from the Water Tower, is a bar hopper's paradise.

3 UNFOLD FOR MAP

MAGNIFICENT MILE

⭐ SIGHTS pp. 1-28

B2
- JOHN HANCOCK CENTER, p. 16
- WATER TOWER, p. 26

B3
- MUSEUM OF CONTEMPORARY ART, p. 18

D6
- NAVY PIER, p. 20

E2
- CHICAGO RIVER BRIDGES (MICHIGAN AVENUE BRIDGE), p. 8

Ⓡ RESTAURANTS pp. 29-42

A1
- GIBSONS STEAKHOUSE, p. 34
- LE COLONIAL, p. 36
- THE ORIGINAL PANCAKE HOUSE, p. 38

A2
- SPIAGGIA, p. 40

B1
- TEMPO CAFE, p. 41

B2
- CHICAGO FLAT SAMMIES, p. 33
- MIKE DITKA'S RESTAURANT, p. 37
- NOMI, p. 38
- SEASONS, p. 40

- SIGNATURE ROOM AT THE 95TH, p. 40
- WOLF & KETTLE COFFEE SHOP, p. 42

C2
- LES NOMADES, p. 36
- SHANGHAI TERRACE, p. 40
- TRU, p. 42

C4
- WAVE, p. 42

D1
- PIZZERIA UNO, p. 39
- SHAW'S CRAB HOUSE, p. 40

D2
- BILLY GOAT TAVERN, p. 32

Ⓢ SHOPS pp. 43-54

A1
- ALTERNATIVES, p. 46
- DAISY SHOP, p. 48
- MADISON & FRIENDS, p. 51
- TENDER BUTTONS, p. 53

A2
- ALEX SEPKUS, p. 46
- GISELA, p. 49
- KATE SPADE, p. 50
- TRUEFITT & HILL, p. 54
- ULTIMO, p. 54

MAP LEGEND

⭐	SIGHTS		DAYTIME HOT SPOTS
Ⓛ	EL STOP		NIGHTTIME HOT SPOTS
Ⓜ	METRA STOP		DAY AND NIGHT
⑤	ADJACENT MAP	- - - - -	CLOSED TO TRAFFIC

Approximate distance across map: 1.25 mi

0   0.25 mile

0   0.25 kilometer

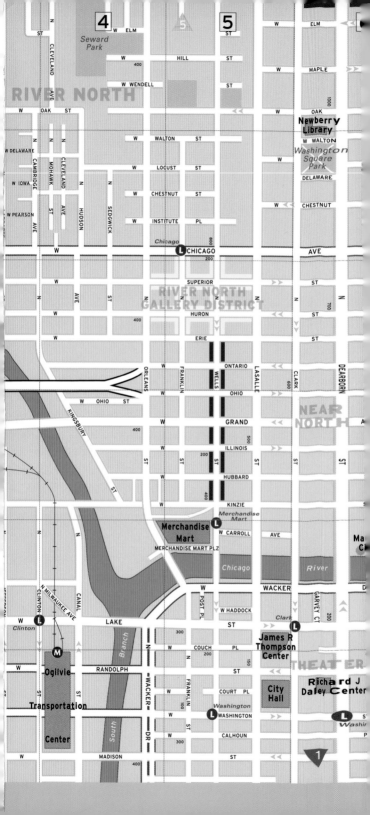

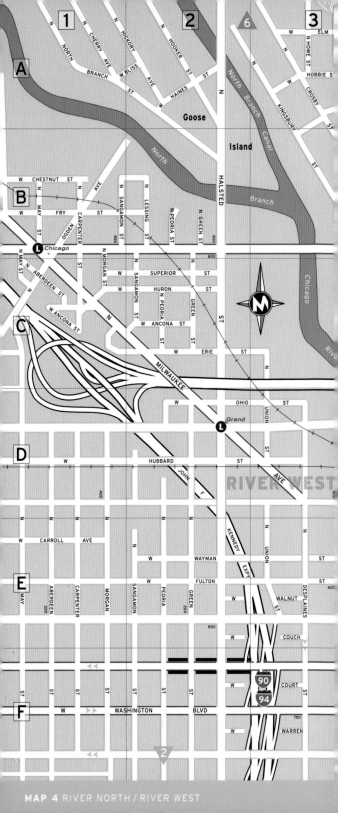

MAP 4 RIVER NORTH / RIVER WEST

RIVER NORTH / RIVER WEST

An art-scene hub by day and dine-and-dance destination by night, the area north of the Chicago River fork holds diversions for serious gallery-goers and bar-hopping gourmands alike.

Once a shaky industrial zone of warehouses and factories, River North experienced a transition in the 1970s, most notably with the population of art galleries growing and concentrating around Superior and Franklin Streets. Today, the area is the River North Gallery District, boasting more than 60 display spaces within a few blocks.

For nighttime denizens, River North sparkles after sunset, even as the rest of the Loop turns into an urban ghost town. Bright and busy, this hot spot, with its assemblage of bars, clubs, and popular eateries, is your best bet for an evening out and a million cabs eager to take you home at the end of it.

On River North's restaurant rows, garish locales, like the Rainforest and Hard Rock Cafes, share space with more unique diners and bistros. The '50s-style Ed Debevic's prides itself on its cartoonish rudeness and Maggiano's Little Italy will serve up a gut-busting meal. Gene & Georgetti claims the title of Chicago's oldest steakhouse – no small feat in this carnivorous town – and while McDonalds are every-

 where, the one-of-a-kind Rock 'n Roll branch on Clark Street pays tribute to the chain's Midwestern roots. After all the eats, the nearby watering holes, dance spots, and music venues give visitors a chance to either work off their dinner or enjoy a change of scenery as they digest.

At the southern tip of River North are Marina City's two giant corn cob-shaped towers, which at one point were the

MAP 4 RIVER NORTH / RIVER WEST

MAP 4

tallest residential and tallest concrete structures in the world. At the base of Marina City is the House of Blues chain where big music stars play in the club and Southern cooking is doled out in the downstairs restaurant. On the other end of Kinzie, right at the river's fork, the Merchandise Mart will satisfy those in town with a taste for the cushy stuff. Homemakers can shop for designer furniture and fancy decorations in this large commercial building. At the very least, couch testing grants an excuse to relax before heading out for a bite.

Across the river, River West sports some pockets of activity, but not to the same degree as its northern counterpart. Straddling the vague boundary between River West and the West Loop, the bustling strip of trendy restaurants on Randolph Street, featuring the white-hot Marché and Sushi Wabi, teems with double-parked luxury cars lined up in front of the exclusive eateries. Otherwise, some of the surrounding neighborhood can get pretty shabby, and although it's still safe, visitors should remain aware.

River West is also a gateway to other attractions outside the area. Although it is located in a grungy part of town, the United Center (1901 W. Madison Street) remains a popular destination, since the west-side arena is where Michael Jordan once led the Bulls to so many national championships. And if you were to follow Chicago Avenue nine miles away from the city center (although the CTA Green Line may be a better bet), you'd find Oak Park where Frank Lloyd Wright once lived and left his mark.

 UNFOLD FOR MAP

RIVER NORTH / RIVER WEST

MAP LEGEND

★	SIGHTS		DAYTIME HOT SPOTS
ⓛ	EL STOP		NIGHTTIME HOT SPOTS
ⓜ	METRA STOP		DAY AND NIGHT
▽5	ADJACENT MAP	- - -	CLOSED TO TRAFFIC

Approximate distance across map: 1.7 mi

0   0.25 mile

0   0.25 kilometer

PKY
N COMMONWEALTH
PKY

Conservatory

LINCOLN

PARK

WEST

300

N ORLEANS ST

CLARK

AVE

N NORTH ST

PARK AVE

N CRILLY

MENOMONEE ST

WILLOW ST

ST ST

N ORLEANS ST

W ST. PAUL AVE

CT

EUGENIE

200

ICORD PL

JOHN

C

**LINCOLN PARK/
LINCOLN PARK ZOO**

STOCKTON

CANNON

RIDGE DR

DR

South
Pond

DR

RIDGE

DR

LASALLE

N

DR

CANNON

DR

Lincoln

Park

LAKE

MICHIGA

41

N LAKE SHORE

North Ave
Beach

**Chicago
Historical
Society**

E NORTH BLVD

AVE

N

N

NORTH

ORLEANS

PARK

ST

WIELAND

ST

W GERMANIA

N

SANDBURG

N

1500

BURTON PL

DEARBORN

N

E BURTON PL

STATE

ASTOR

LAKE

SHORE

INNER

DR

M

ST

SCHILLER

W

N

N

1400

E SCHILLER ST

ERGREEN

AVE

AVE

WELLS

LASALLE

100

N SUTTON PL

CLARK

PKY

ST

E BANKS ST

RITCHIE

ST

1300

ST

ST

DR

GOETHE

ST

ST

E GOETHE ST

N STONE ST

W SCOTT ST

200

TER

ST

E SCOTT ST

**GOLD
COAST**

1200

Clark/
Division

L

ST

N FRANKLIN

ST

W ELM ST

E ELM ST

Oa

LM

ORLEANS

ST

HILL

ST

W MAPLE ST

E CEDAR ST

3

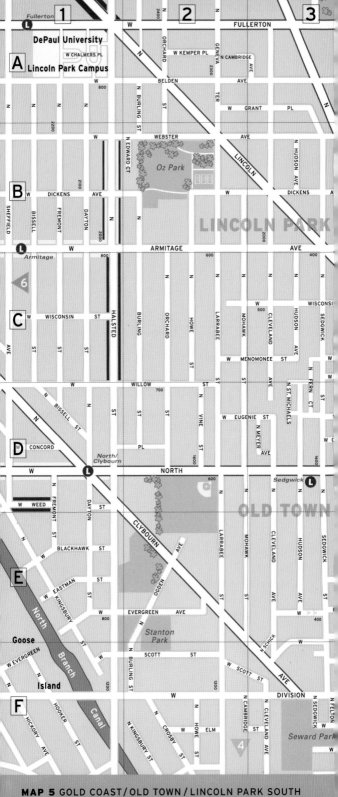

MAP 5 GOLD COAST/OLD TOWN/LINCOLN PARK SOUTH

GOLD COAST/OLD TOWN/ LINCOLN PARK SOUTH

Sometimes the simplest way to get a sense of a particular area in Chicago is the neighborhood's name itself. The Gold Coast, located just north of the similarly illustrative Magnificent Mile, is not a destination for penny pinchers. After a mass South Loop-to-North Side migration in the late 1800s, the Gold Coast became home to many of Chicago's upper crust. Today, fur coats remain in vogue, and if you're looking to splurge, dinner can set you back hundreds of dollars and force you to don your best suit. There's also plenty to look at, if not acquire, for those more inclined to stare than spend.

Gold Coast residents think big. Housing options range from any number of doorman-guarded high-rises to the luxurious town houses that spring up as you move north. The airiness of the neighborhood is a mark of the original planners who made sure to keep some of the land undeveloped once they themselves were comfortably ensconced. Representative of the Gold Coast scene is Oak Street Beach, a little touch of Los Angeles on the shore of Lake Michigan. It's where the well-formed go to sunbathe in view of some of Chicago's most luxurious lakeside skyscrapers and bay-windowed restaurants, assuming they can find room amidst all the summer volleyball players.

Thanks to the Great Fire, little of Chicago dates as far back as in cities like New York, Boston, or Philadelphia. But even though it was forced to make a fresh start, the city still retains some olden-days flavor in areas, one of which is Old Town. A pocket of preserved late 19th-century homes, Old Town originally absorbed a lot of the moneyed spillover from its neighbor to the south, the Gold Coast. The 1960s

MAP 5 GOLD COAST/OLD TOWN/LINCOLN PARK SOUTH

MAP 5

saw an influx of counterculture types, leaving this well-off area with an arty vibe. Smaller buildings and the occasional cobblestone indicate the area's age and affluence; the tree-lined streets and nice homes make Old Town a pleasant place to take a walk. The restaurants along Wells Street – serving everything from ribs to sushi to multicourse meals – lead to North Avenue, where the venerable Second City improv group has been training future *Saturday Night Live* stars for decades.

Bordering Old Town is the Lincoln Park neighborhood, which retains a similarly tony atmosphere. Of particular note is Armitage Avenue, a street lined with diversions from fashion designer Cynthia Rowley's store to Charlie Trotter's world-renowned gourmet restaurant, where a meal that you'll savor for a lifetime will also cost at least a hundred a head. If you wear out your shoes from walking around, there are plenty of funky stores eager to sell you a new pair. Ever more activity can be found at the actual Lincoln Park and its zoo, where you can explore the award-winning exhibits or go paddleboating. Learn about Chicago at the Historical Society, or come summer, just bask in the sun, taking in the overwhelming, but welcome, smell of several picnickers barbecuing simultaneously.

SOUTH

GOLD COAST / OLD TOWN / LINCOLN PARK

★ SIGHTS pp. 1-28

® RESTAURANTS pp. 29-42

⑤ SHOPS pp. 43-54

MAP LEGEND

★ SIGHTS

Ⓛ EL STOP

Ⓜ METRA STOP

5 ADJACENT MAP

DAYTIME HOT SPOTS

NIGHTTIME HOT SPOTS

DAY AND NIGHT

CLOSED TO TRAFFIC

Approximate distance across map: 1.85 mi

0   0.25 mile

0   0.25 kilometer

MAP 6 BUCKTOWN / WICKER PARK

BUCKTOWN / WICKER PARK

Despite their gentrification, the North Side neighborhoods of Bucktown and Wicker Park give off an eclectic, more bohemian vibe than their moneyed Old Town and Gold Coast counterparts. Formerly working class and ethnically diverse, Bucktown and Wicker Park attracted artists and other budget-minded invaders with low rents, big lofts, and nice buildings. The galleries, shops, and restaurants soon followed, catering to a deeper-pocketed crowd who liked the area's burgeoning culture. Higher rents came next, changing the character of the neighborhoods by pricing out many of its longtime residents.

Even after this cultural shift, both areas still remain more diverse than most Chicago neighborhoods, welcoming professionals and students alike to share in the cultural offerings. Bucktown has become the more exclusive of the two, drawing the city's yuppie elite with its wide selection of boutiques, wine bars, and restaurants. Perfect places to cool off after an afternoon of window-shopping, Bucktown cafés feature fenced-in back patios that come alive in the summer. Hidden on Wabansia near the river is one of Chicago's friendliest country bars, the well-named Hideout, a favorite with local music lovers. The impressive St. Mary of the Angels Church at Hermitage and Cortland retains the link with the Polish immigrants who originally built the neighborhood.

The physical Wicker Park is located just a couple blocks from the Damen El stop, which serves as the neighborhood's central hub. When MTV finally tapped Chicago for a season of *The Real World,* the producers picked Wicker Park as the place to put the pretty cast. No wonder: the neighborhood is teeming with all that attracts the young and hip. New record

MAP 6 BUCKTOWN / WICKER PARK

MAP 6

stores and quirky restaurants continue to pop up, while laughter wafts from dozens of clubs and bars until the wee hours. A sushi dinner can be topped off with a night of free jazz, or an eccentric southern fusion at Soul Kitchen can be followed by a major touring rock act next door at Double Door, where several of Chicago's biggest names often play surprise shows. A multitude of bookstores and clothing shops beckon browsers, though the shelves of Quimby's comic bookstore and the French pastry shop Sweet Thang attract a more specific clientele.

Wicker Park survived the Great Chicago Fire unscathed, and so did its history. Several grand houses stand among the newer condos and townhouses as testaments to Chicago's rich past, each with their own attributes. Writer Nelson Algren's house remains intact, though not open to the public. Many of Wicker Park's early 20th-century mansions mark Chicago's various renovation runs by their lack of the same: sunken lawns signify the days before Chicago raised its street levels, and the wood-framed homes betray their age since they had to have been constructed before fire codes forbade easily flammable materials.

The perfect place to spend a warm afternoon, Wicker Park and Bucktown both feature enough nooks and crannies to satisfy residents and visitors alike. The only limit to the many activities and distractions is time. The relatively neat boundaries make walking the neighborhoods an easy task and the character of the area promises some colorful adventure.

BUCKTOWN / WICKER PARK

Wicker Park

an historic neighborhood
miejska dzielnica historyczna
vecindario histórico

MAP LEGEND

⭐	SIGHTS	DAYTIME HOT SPOTS
Ⓛ	EL STOP	NIGHTTIME HOT SPOTS
Ⓜ	METRA STOP	DAY AND NIGHT
5	ADJACENT MAP	- - - - - CLOSED TO TRAFFIC

Approximate distance across map: 2 mi

0 ————— 0.25 mile

0 ————— 0.25 kilometer

LAKE VIEW/LINCOLN PARK NORTH

One of the greatest beneficiaries of Chicago's urban renewal streak in the late 1970s, the North Side Lake View/Lincoln Park area attracts a diverse mix of residents with its picturesque location near the lake. The popularity of the neighborhoods is reflected in one of the city's most pressing parking crunches, particularly in Lake View, which swarms with day-trippers whenever the Cubs return home to Wrigley Field. Half the traffic seems to be taken up by cars circling incessantly, in search of that elusive unrestricted street spot.

While the ballpark is Lake View's central attraction, it is accompanied by a bevy of bars and shops that cater to the neighborhood's broad makeup and support the party atmosphere of game day. Close to Wrigley Field are many rambunctious sports bars that open out onto crowded sidewalks. Many provide exclusive rooftop game vantages for those who arrive early enough (and for those willing to pay the right price).

Just a few blocks east is the predominantly gay North Halsted strip known as Boystown, a street delineated with rainbow-ringed towers, which also mark the colorful starting point for the annual summer pride parade. There's also a strong selection of nightclubs and great places to eat, ranging from pancake houses to tasty French-Asian fusion.

Tattoo parlors and cheap eateries abound around the intersection of Clark and Belmont, attracting young suburban interlopers with a combination of decadent shops and grungy atmosphere. Here, Indian buffets mingle with hamburger joints and smoothie stands, and this is the place to go for a leather jacket and a dozen donuts. The closer you move toward the lake, the cleaner the action gets, although it retains the same variety of restaurants, especially Asian cuisine, and stores.

MAP 7 LAKE VIEW/LINCOLN PARK NORTH

MAP 7

The north end of tidy, affluent Lincoln Park is also filled with unique shops, restaurants, and activities. On Lincoln Avenue the famous Biograph Theater, where John Dillinger met his end, screens film festivals and other special events. Dog lovers should head to the cute Wiggly Field to let their pets loose amongst tail-wagging friends. Nearby Halsted Street features some familiar clothing stores interspersed with exclusive boutiques that service a well-off clientele. You can spend an afternoon watching a league softball game at one of many serene parks, admiring the boats at Belmont Harbor, or enjoying the daredevil skateboarders who gather after school to show off their stunts. Few Chicago neighborhoods are as conducive to relaxation, and while you'll never forget that you're in the middle of a city (the always-visible Sears Tower prevents that), the tree-lined streets and numerous benches beckon you to grab a coffee and take a break.

Of course, excitement is there for those who want it. Some Lincoln Park clubs and bars give Lake View a run for its money, and restaurants and local watering holes fill up fast on the weekends. But for the most part, Lincoln Park is a good place to wind up a day rather than begin a long night.

LAKE VIEW / LINCOLN PARK NORTH

MAP LEGEND

★	SIGHTS		DAYTIME HOT SPOTS
Ⓛ	EL STOP		NIGHTTIME HOT SPOTS
Ⓜ	METRA STOP		DAY AND NIGHT
5	ADJACENT MAP	-----	CLOSED TO TRAFFIC

Approximate distance across map: 2.25 mi

0   0.25 mile

0   0.25 kilometer

South Branch Chicago River

LUMBER

1

2

W 13TH S

FEDERAL

S PLYMOUTH

E 13TH S >> 13TH ST

3

1300

A

W 14TH ST

ST

CT

E

E 14TH ST

200

14TH

1400

S

E 14TH PL

W 15TH ST

1500

S

S

S

CLARK

ST

B

W 16TH ST

1600

16TH

S

SO

W 17TH

1700

FEDERAL

DEARBORN

ST

S

W 18TH ST

1800

E 18TH

18TH

1900

100

C

ST

W 19TH ST

STATE

HOLDEN

WABASH

MICHIGAN

INDIANA

AVE

ARCHER

W CULLERTON ST

E

CULLERTON

ST

200

TAN CT

W CULLERTON

S WELLS ST

CHINA PL

S

2000

S

S

ST

E

21ST

2100

Cermak/Chinatown

CT

E

D

W CERMAK M RD E CERMAK

2200

CHINATOWN

W 22ND PL

WENTWORTH

S

E

W ALEXANDER ST

W 23RD ST

23RD

2300

E

23RD

AVE

AVE

AVE

100

PRINCETON

W 23RD PL

AVE

FEDERAL

DEARBORN

ST

W 24TH ST

200

W 24TH ST

E

24TH

ST

2400

ST

W 25TH ST

STEVENSON

E 25TH

5

AVE

ADLAI

E

F

W 25TH PL

ST

25TH PL

DAN RYAN EXPY

PRINCETON

WELLS

W 26TH ST

S LA SALLE ST

FEDERAL

DEARBORN

ST

2500

26TH

ST

WABASH

AVE

100

S INDIANA AVE

W 27TH ST

W 27TH ST

ST

MAP 8 SOUTH LOOP/BURNHAM PARK

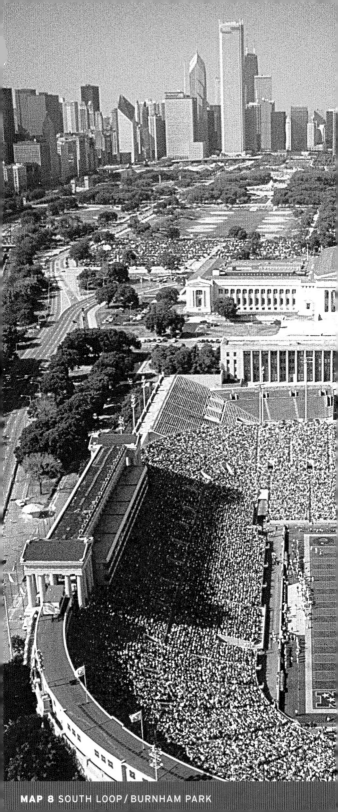

MAP 8 SOUTH LOOP / BURNHAM PARK

MAP 8

SOUTH LOOP / BURNHAM PARK

Partly due to its notorious reputation as a dangerous neighborhood, the South Loop didn't see a revitalization until late in the 20th century. But those prescient enough to invest early have reaped the benefits of one of Chicago's most impressive housing booms. Condos are going up as fast as the old warehouses can be converted, and older buildings, like the original Chess Records (legendary for its contributions to blues and rock-and-roll), are all but invisible amongst the new construction. Between all this development and the neighborhood presence of Mayor Richard M. Daley, this district could be headed back on top.

Right by the lake is Soldier Field, the Bears' giant outdoor stadium, which, too, is undergoing a complete renovation, much to the dismay of Bears traditionalists. Nearby, occasional air traffic passes through the controversial Meigs Field, used mostly by state politicians and businessmen.

Further south, the Prairie Avenue Historic District covers a few square blocks with the city's oldest homes, many of which date back to the mid-1800s when the South Loop was the place to be if you had money and power. Straddling Lake Shore Drive, McCormick Place, the United States' largest convention center, dominates the area. Chinatown stretches along Wentworth below Cermak, although the relatively small selection of restaurants and shops pales in comparison to its East and West Coast cousins.

On a map the South Loop doesn't seem that far from the center of downtown, but the distances can be deceptive. What might appear on paper to be a short stroll could in fact take a lot longer. And while buses and the El run along set paths, catching a cab can be tough, so plan accordingly.

SOUTH LOOP/BURNHAM PARK

⭐ SIGHTS pp. 1-28

MAP LEGEND

⭐	SIGHTS		DAYTIME HOT SPOTS
Ⓛ	EL STOP	▬▬	NIGHTTIME HOT SPOTS
Ⓜ	METRA STOP	▬▬	DAY AND NIGHT
5	ADJACENT MAP	- - - -	CLOSED TO TRAFFIC

Approximate distance across map: 1.7 mi

0   0.25 mile

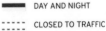

0   0.25 kilometer

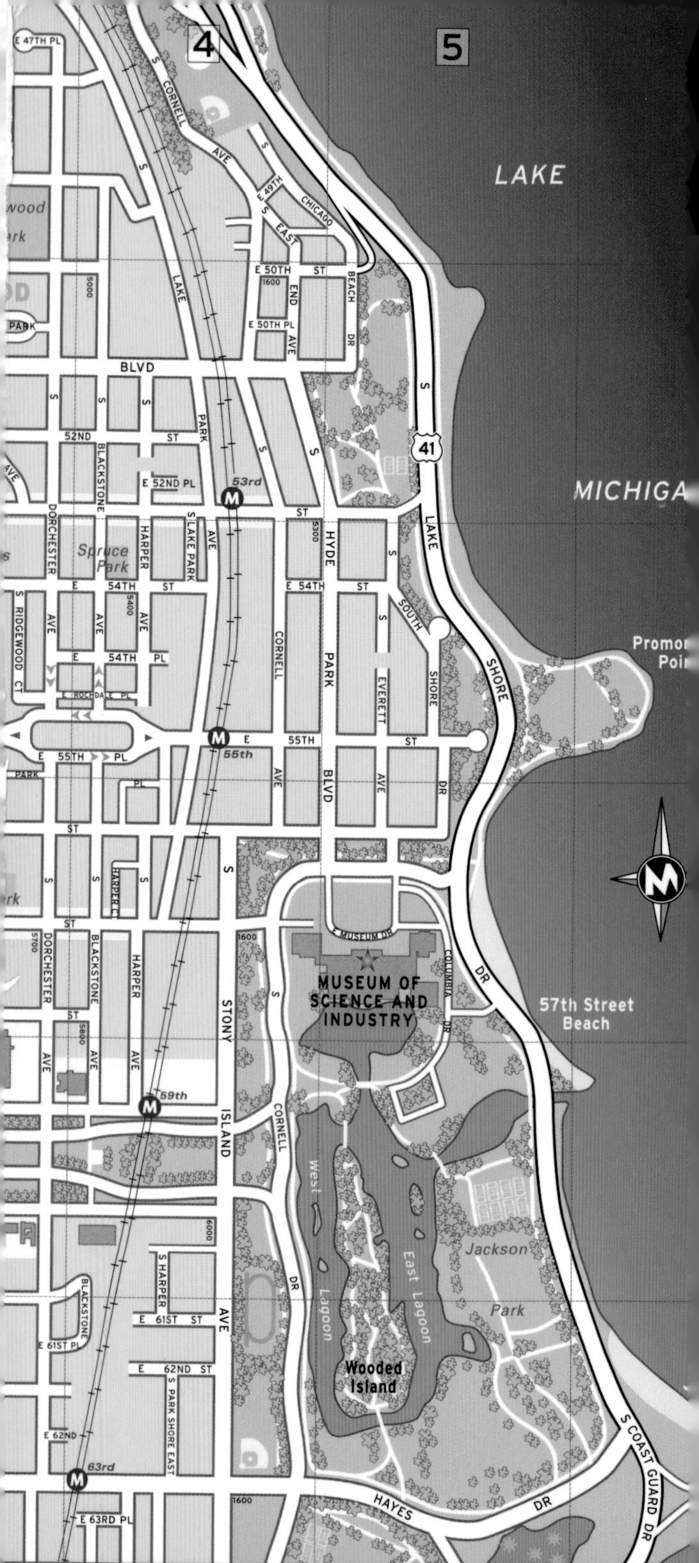

E 47TH PL

CORNELL AVE

S 49TH

CHICAGO

EAST

LAKE

E 50TH ST

1600

END AVE

BEACH DR

E 50TH PL

wood Park

BLVD

PARK

52ND ST

BLACKSTONE

DORCHESTER

RIDGEWOOD CT

E 52ND PL

53rd

HYDE

5500

M

LAKE

S LAKE PARK AVE

HARPER AVE

5400

E 54TH ST

E 54TH PL

CORNELL AVE

PARK

E 55TH PL

PARK

ST

DORCHESTER

BLACKSTONE

5700

HARPER

5800

Spruce Park

Ridgewood Ct

E

M E 55th

E 55TH

BLVD

EVERETT AVE

M 59th

STONY ISLAND

CORNELL

1600

MUSEUM DR

MUSEUM OF SCIENCE AND INDUSTRY

COLUMBIA DR

LAKE

SOUTH

SHORE

DR

41

LAKE

MICHIGA

Promor Poi

M

57th Street Beach

West Lagoon

East Lagoon

Jackson Park

S HARPER AVE

E 61ST ST

E 61ST PL

E 62ND ST

S PARK SHORE EAST

E 62ND

6000

M 63rd

E 63RD PL

1600

DR

Wooded Island

HAYES DR

S COAST GUARD DR

5000

5100

5000

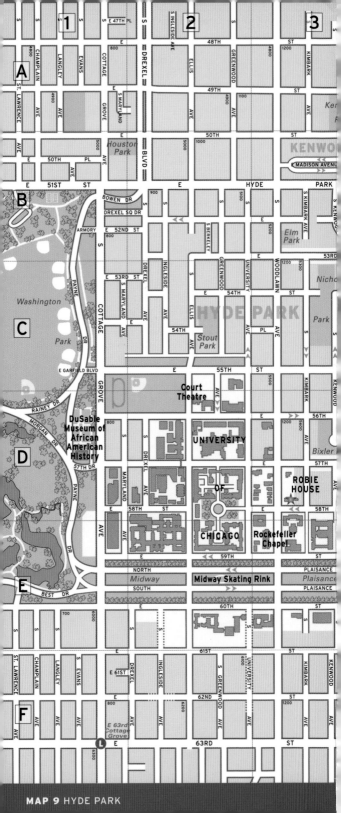

MAP 9 HYDE PARK

MAP 9

HYDE PARK

At one point in time, Hyde Park contained some of the South Side's most exciting jazz clubs and blues bars, making it a vibrant center of African American culture in a city sadly more segregated than most. Yet in the '50s and '60s, the combined efforts of local government and the University of Chicago to dry out the neighborhood drove out many of the great nightlife venues, and soon after parts of Hyde Park fell into disrepair. One of the few reminders of Hyde Park's one-time prosperity is the string of huge houses – large mansions with big yards at odds with the usual tight confines of the city – at the neighborhood's north end.

Keeping Hyde Park's decline in check was the university. Its campus still serves as one of the community's most prominent employers, and it also brings an annual influx of students eager to explore. The neo-Gothic campus itself features the well-kept grounds that mark most campuses, though the sheer number of coffeeshops-cum-study halls sets it apart from the average party school. Carillon bells ring out regularly from Rockefeller Chapel, a short distance from Frank Lloyd Wright's Prairie-style Robie House.

The rest of Hyde Park is mostly residential, with families attracted by the schools and affordable housing. A number of great museums – most notably the popular Museum of Science and Industry – and theaters are spread throughout Hyde Park, though the neighborhood's restaurant rows are centered on 53rd and 57th Streets.

Visitors should be aware that public transportation service in this area is spotty and despite the pronounced presence of the University's private police force, the neighborhood doesn't lend itself very well to nocturnal tours.

UNFOLD FOR MAP

MAP 9 HYDE PARK

HYDE PARK

⭐ SIGHTS pp. 1-28

ⓡ RESTAURANTS pp. 29-42

ⓢ SHOPS pp. 43-54

MAP LEGEND

⭐	SIGHTS		DAYTIME HOT SPOTS
ⓛ	EL STOP		NIGHTTIME HOT SPOTS
ⓜ	METRA STOP		DAY AND NIGHT
🔻5	ADJACENT MAP	- - - - -	CLOSED TO TRAFFIC

Approximate distance across map: 2.25 mi

0   0.25 mile

0   0.25 kilometer

⊛ **SIGHTS**

ADLER PLANETARIUM AND ASTRONOMY MUSEUM

Chicago's lakeside location generally keeps the skies clear, but as with all big cities, the bright lights at night prevent stargazers from viewing all their favorite celestial sights. Fortunately, Chicago boasts the perfect method for circumventing the glowing electrical glare: the Adler Planetarium. Situated on the city's popular Museum Campus right on the shore of Lake Michigan, the planetarium shares the research-minded bent of its neighbors, the Field Museum and the Shedd Aquarium. Similarly, the Adler Planetarium goes a long way to make astronomical science accessible for people of all ages and knowledge levels.

Chicago businessman Max Adler founded the museum in 1930, centering the collection around the planetarium's Zeiss projector. Adler filled the planetarium with hundreds of astronomy artifacts and instruments — some dating back to the 12th century — that range from relatively primitive sundials to state-of-the-art telescopes. Today, boasting more than 2,000 such items as well as hundreds of rare books, the Adler Planetarium is one of the largest and most important museums of its type.

In addition to displaying its permanent collections, the museum mounts numerous themed exhibits, which have in the past focused on celestial interests such as comets, constellations, and calendars, plus numerous pioneering astronomers and their discoveries. Then, of course, there's the Zeiss projector, that familiar planetarium fixture capable of projecting thousands of stars, suns, and other extraterrestrial bodies onto the museum's domed auditorium ceiling, submerging visitors in a blissful darkness punctuated by the pinpricks of light beamed above.

For those interested in the real thing as well as the simulation, the Adler Planetarium also features the Doane Observatory. Completed in 1977, it enlists a 500-pound telescope with a 20-inch cassegrain reflector lens to search the skies. Chicago never seems as small as it does when you're staring out into millions of miles of space.

 F6 1300 S. LAKE SHORE DR. 312-922-7827
HOURS: MON.-SUN. 9:30 A.M.-4:30 P.M.; EXTENDED HOURS FIRST FRIDAY OF EVERY MONTH 5-10 P.M.

ART INSTITUTE OF CHICAGO

Virtually every large metropolitan city has its art museum, but given the relatively finite number of great works in existence, not every collection is a must-see. This is certainly not the case with the Art Institute of Chicago. Even the museum-averse will find much to love (and recognize) in the stunning selection of famous and familiar works that run the gamut from primitive sculptures to playfully surreal modern pieces.

Designed by the team of Shepley, Rutan, and Coolidge, the imposing building was constructed in 1893 for the World's Columbian Exposition. Inside, the Art Institute houses more than 300,000 invaluable works, including one of the world's greatest assemblages of Impressionist art.

Notables from the permanent collection include such American classics as Grant Wood's 1930 *American Gothic* and Edward Hopper's 1942 *Nighthawks*, though both have been referenced and parodied so many times that the originals seem rather modest. On display in the European Painting gallery is Georges Seurat's *Sunday Afternoon on the Island Grande Jatte*, giving visitors an amazing up-close view of his detailed, pointillist painting style. And just as the Art Institute commonly lends out pieces from its collections (its 33 works by Monet are the envy of many), the museum regularly hosts popular touring exhibits from around the world.

Long hours make the Art Institute easy to visit and encourage a leisurely stroll through the well-organized collections. But even as visitors circulate, the next generation of artists is honing its talents right around the corner. The actual School of the Art Institute faces Columbus Drive, though its stellar movie theater, which specializes in classic and foreign films, has been moved to State Street and renamed the Gene Siskel Film Center in honor of the late *Chicago Tribune* film critic.

 B2 111 S. MICHIGAN AVE. 312-443-3600
HOURS: MON., WED.-FRI. 10:30 A.M.-4:30 P.M., TUES. 10:30 A.M.-8 P.M., SAT.-SUN. 10 A.M.-5 P.M.

CHICAGO BOARD OF TRADE

In the mid-1800s, the Chicago Board of Trade was devised to organize the grain trade, making it the oldest futures exchange in the world. Besides the chaotic open-outcry floor filled with traders, CBOT is known for the building's dramatic architecture, showing off its status as a major Midwestern center of commerce in the heart of the Loop's financial district.

Practice makes perfect when it comes to the evolution of the building's architecture. In 1928, the exchange commissioned the firm of Holabird and Root to design the current edition of the Board of Trade, and the building has endured as a functional Chicago landmark. An eye-catching art deco structure of limestone and glass, the CBOT building was completed in 1930, but predictably more refinements followed. Thirteen-story wings were added to comply with zoning ordinances, and sculptor John Storrs topped the building with a 31-foot, three-and-a-quarter ton aluminum statue of Ceres, the Roman goddess of grain and harvest. The north-facing exterior also displays several agricultural symbols surrounding a large inset clock.

Security concerns have kept the Visitor Center, and its windows on the trading floor, closed to the general public, but regular neighborhood tours allow a memorable glimpse at the workmanship of this grand collision of art and business.

 C5 141 W. JACKSON BLVD. 312-435-3590
CALL FOR UPDATED VISITOR CENTER ACCESS INFORMATION.

SIDE WALKS

• Coffee and a muffin at Gourmand
D6 728 S. DEARBORN ST. 312-427-2610

• The Rookery's Frank Lloyd Wright–designed lobby
C5 209 S. LASALLE ST.

• Printer's Row Historic District and the *History of Printing* mural
D6 720 S. DEARBORN ST.

• An evening out in the Theater District
A6 HOT TIX: 78 W. RANDOLPH ST.

CHICAGO CULTURAL CENTER

Convenient to public transportation and downtown hotels, the well-situated Chicago Cultural Center is a great starting place for first-time visitors to the Windy City – the Chicago Office of Tourism's Visitor Information Center is located on the first floor. But while its staff can surely help you find your way to other attractions around the city, there's actually plenty to see inside the Cultural Center itself.

Completed in 1897 to serve as the city's original public library, the center was designed by the same architecture team that worked on the Art Institute. The building's columns and use of open space are styled in the vein of classic Greek and Roman structures. On the other hand, the beautiful interiors recall the opulent splendors of Venice and Florence, featuring grand staircases and two sparkling glass domes, one in the Grand Army of the Republic Rotunda and the other – a Tiffany production valued at more than $35 million – in the Preston Bradley Hall. Less ostentatious are the numerous mosaics, slick marble embellishments, and engraved quotations that call out to be discovered by the curious.

As to be expected, the arts get generous treatment inside the center. The permanent Museum of Broadcast Communications offers a pleasant trip down radio and television memory lane, while three regularly changing spaces showcase works from up-and-coming artists and traveling international exhibits alike. In addition to the visual arts, the building dedicates space to the performing arts in its Dance Studio, Claudia Cassidy Theater, Studio Theater, and grand Preston Bradley Hall.

Unlike many other major landmarks, the Cultural Center is one place where tourists and locals regularly mingle. Be sure to check out the center's calendar of current events, since it frequently hosts several great festivals and one-time-only attractions, from films and lectures to portions of the annual Asian American Jazz Festival and the World Music Festival. Ever functional, the Cultural Center offers up its space for weddings every Saturday morning, and it also attracts a busy lunchtime crowd with free noontime music.

 A2 78 E. WASHINGTON ST. 312-346-3278
HOURS: MON.-WED. 10 A.M.-7 P.M., THURS. 10 A.M.-9 P.M., FRI. 10 A.M.-6 P.M., SAT. 10 A.M.-5 P.M., SUN. 11 A.M.-5 P.M.

CHICAGO RIVER BRIDGES

Bisecting the city, the Chicago River essentially served as Chicago's first major highway, allowing the region to flourish as a regional center of trade. Potawatomi Indian pelt peddlers regularly made the rounds up and down the river, interacting with early settlers who understood how the water route made the land desirable. As time passed, the value of the Chicago River only increased, and with the advance of technology the entire river system improved as well.

In 1900, thanks to an impressive feat of engineering, the city actually reversed the flow of the river, forcing it to run away from the lake to protect the city's clean water supply. In addition, to better serve the arrival of larger trade ships, the city dredged the river deeper and built a number of bridges downtown.

While many of Chicago's bridges feature unique designs and applications, the most impressive are the various trunnion bascule drawbridges, named for the system of pivots and counterweights that raise and lower the heavy platforms. Chicago actually has more moveable bridges than anywhere else in the world, and while harried commuters typically dread running into one of the raised bridges, visitors are in for a treat.

The Cortland Street Bridge, engineered in 1902 by John Ernst Ericson, was the first trunnion bascule built in the United States, and the red steel structure remains impressive. The mammoth Michigan Avenue Bridge provides even more pleasures, as it's bracketed by two large sculptures. Slightly away from the center of things is the award-winning, steel-arch Damen Avenue Bridge. Lined with ribbons of red and located just a few miles west of downtown Chicago, the bridge is a more modern addition to Chicago's tradition.

OVERVIEW MAP B3 DAMEN AVENUE BRIDGE: N. DAMEN AVE. AT CHICAGO RIVER

 E2 MICHIGAN AVENUE BRIDGE: MICHIGAN AVE. AT CHICAGO RIVER

 C4 CORTLAND STREET BRIDGE: 1440 W. CORTLAND ST.

CHICAGO THEATER

For several years it looked as if the Chicago Theater would just languish unused. Centrally located in one of the city's busiest areas, the theater passed from owner to owner, none of whom apparently wanted to put in the necessary work to restoring the landmark. Fortunately, financial issues were eventually sorted out, and the theater was finally fixed up, and anyone who has seen the theater's interior will wonder how anyone could have waited so long to return the old movie house to its original luster.

Built in the 1920s, in the time of great movie houses, the 3,800-seat Chicago Theater cost an impressive $2 million to build, but the architectural firm of Rapp & Rapp made every penny worthwhile. The building's classic revival/beaux-arts style makes visitors feel like they've gone back in time. Not only does the theater recall the pre-Depression days of sophisticated urban extravagance, it was designed to resemble the Palace of Versailles's Mansarts Chapel. The five-story lobby features gilded walls and red carpets and is lined with Stueben glass light fixtures. Moviegoing probably never seemed so regal.

The thorough renovation of the Chicago Theater greatly increased its versatility. Once strictly a cinema that drew millions of visitors a year, it now brings in huge touring acts and stage productions. The staff likes to recount the concert by the British rock band Oasis — it was so loud that the lobby's ceiling shook dramatically. Those in search of more stories can opt for the affordable and informative guided tour. For a $5 fee that benefits renovation costs, visitors can spy on the dressing rooms and see the legendary backstage walls, autographed by everyone from Frank Sinatra to Sting. You're also offered a view of the auditorium from the stage itself, an exclusive vantage usually only enjoyed by the world's top entertainers.

 A6 175 N. STATE ST. 312-263-1138

FIELD MUSEUM OF NATURAL HISTORY

The Field Museum of Natural History may be one of the few attractions known as much for what's not on display as for what is. The museum's legendary underground storage area holds 250,000 volumes on the history of the Earth and upwards of 20 million crate-bound curios from around the world, each catalogued and set aside for study when not out for all to see.

Like that of many Chicago museums and landmarks, the Field Museum's inception coincided with the 1893 Columbian Exposition. (In fact, before it was renamed in 1905 to honor benefactor Marshall Field, it was known as the Columbian Museum of Chicago.) Originally focused on biological and anthropological collections, the Field Museum grows more and more impressive with each acquisition. In 2000, the museum garnered still more international attention when it debuted Sue, the largest, most complete, and best preserved *Tyrannosaurus rex* fossil ever discovered. That massive skeleton alone draws thousands to the site.

The crowd-pleasing Sue, whose skull is so heavy it needs its own separate support, stands on the second floor, surrounded by *T. rex* facts. But beyond the big dinosaur is a huge warehouse of other discoveries designed to appeal to patrons of all ages. Permanent exhibits exploring Africa and Asia trace the culture and environment of those other continents with life-size dioramas while the Rocks and Fossils exhibit captures the buried progress of the earth itself. The museum unveils new items and collections all the time, and special events (like their Chocolate Exhibit) bring regular visitors back for another helping.

Once located in the South Side Jackson Park, the Field Museum joined the John G. Shedd Aquarium and the Adler Planetarium to form the city's famed lakeside Museum Campus in 1921. The trio comprises one of the world's most respected centers of learning and science, and its status translates into hours of curious distraction and painless education.

F4 1400 S. LAKE SHORE DR. 312-922-9410
HOURS: MON.-FRI. 10 A.M.-5 P.M., SAT. AND SUN. 9 A.M.-5 P.M. (LABOR DAY-MEMORIAL DAY); DAILY 9 A.M.-5 P.M. (MEMORIAL DAY-LABOR DAY)

GRANT PARK

Situated roughly in the center of Chicago's long lakefront, with the towering skyline as a backdrop and its landmark fountain, Grant Park is hailed as Chicago's "front yard."

The idea for the park began as early as the 1830s, when the section of land was preserved as open space. The park, named after the 18th president, started to take its present form nearly a century later, after it served as a landfill following the 1871 fire. (Its foundation is actually comprised of rubble left over from the Great Fire.) The city revitalized the grounds before the 1994 World Cup Tournament and ever since, Grant Park has been one of Chicago's prime summer spots.

The park stretches out from Michigan Avenue to the lake, between Randolph Street and the Museum Campus. Its centerpiece is Versailles-inspired Buckingham Fountain. Its distinctive pink marble makes the fount one of Chicago's most recognizable sights. The rest of the park, blooming with gardens and green space, documents a diverse hodge-podge of Illinois history. Ivan Mestrovic's 1928 statues *The Bowman* and *The Spearman* pay tribute to the state's former Native American residents, while one of Augustus Saint-Gaudens' two Chicago statues of Abraham Lincoln honors Illinois's favorite son.

Every summer the Chicago Symphony plays at the Petrillo Music Shell, while hundreds of food vendors from around the city gather in Grant Park for the Taste of Chicago in the days leading up to the Fourth of July. The closer to the Fourth it is, the more crowded it gets, with more than a million people eventually arriving to watch the fireworks display.

 E3 337 E. RANDOLPH ST. 312-742-7648

SIDE WALKS

• Museum of Contemporary Photography
  D2 600 S. MICHIGAN AVE. 312-663-5554
• Check out the metalwork façade of Carson Pirie Scott's flagship store
B2 1 S. STATE ST. 312-641-7000
• Browse architecture tomes at Prairie Avenue Bookshop
  C2 418 S. WABASH AVE. 312-922-8311
• Caviar at Russian Tea Time
  B2 77 E. ADAMS ST. 312-360-0000

HAROLD WASHINGTON LIBRARY

 When Chicago's public library collections outgrew their space in the building that is now the Cultural Center, the city opted to rethink the library from the ground up. The result was the 1991 Harold Washington Library, named after Chicago's first African American mayor. Measured at 756,640 square feet in area, it immediately earned a place in the *Guinness Book of World Records* as the largest public library building in the world.

Rooms spilling over with books is all anyone can really ask of a library, but the city went one step further and envisioned a structure that would add to not only the city's educational standing but also to its architectural reputation. The firm of Hammond, Beeby, and Babka took on this task after winning the city's design contest. The building's references to Greek and Roman architecture fit in with the tone of Chicago's great edifices, but its redbrick walls make the library stand out from the other landmarks in its crowded downtown location. Five-story arched windows stare out from three sides of the building, and in 1993 seven large Midwestern-themed ornaments were added to the roof.

A mural dedicated to the accomplishments of Harold Washington graces the walls of the lobby, and other local works of art can be found throughout the building. Of course, the library's biggest draw is its book collection of roughly nine million volumes and documents that occupy more than 70 miles of shelves. The giant second floor Children's Library takes up a respectable 18,000 square feet, while it's safe to say that the remaining seven floors contain nearly all there is to know in the world. While locals lose themselves in the library for hours, visitors can settle for a comprehensive guided tour packed with enough facts to fill a few books of their own.

 C1 400 S. STATE ST. 312-747-4999
HOURS: MON.-THURS. 9 A.M.-7 P.M., FRI. AND SAT. 9 A.M.-5 P.M., SUN. 1-5 P.M.

JOHN G. SHEDD AQUARIUM

 Part of the trinity of Museum Campus institutions that explore the natural world around us, the Shedd Aquarium, the world's largest indoor aquarium, offers an amazing escape from city life, submerging visitors in several different aquatic environments stocked with exotic fish and animals.

Built using a $3 million bequest from millionaire, and second president of Marshall Field and Company, John G. Shedd, the aquarium opened its doors just two months after the 1929 stock market crash. At the opening, some of the exhibits still lacked their aquatic residents and the Shedd has been steadily improving its offerings ever since.

Upon entering, visitors first come across the Caribbean Reef exhibit, situated in the skylight-lit rotunda. From the rotunda, several distinct wings radiate out like spokes, each dedicated to a specific ecosystem, from the far-flung Amazon to the more quotidian Illinois Lakes and Rivers. Of particular note is the fascinating seahorse exhibit, which not only sheds some much needed light on these strange creatures, but also explains their plight at the hands of poachers. The exhibit includes a bevy of other bizarre seahorse relatives, such as the skinny pipefish and the wild-looking dragonfish.

The aquarium's most striking attribute is its dolphin and beluga whale exhibits, located in the Oceanarium downstairs. A wide, concave window that looks out over the lake borders the simulated Pacific Coast environment. When the weather cooperates, the lake makes the tank look like it extends out for miles, an inspiring illusion. No doubt the dolphins themselves aren't fooled, since their regular performances − when trainers coax a variety of tricks from the animals − demonstrate just how smart the sea mammals are. Say hello to the friendly creatures from one of the underwater viewing booths, or stay topside and study the unfailingly cute sea otters as they play.

 F4 1200 S. LAKE SHORE DR. 312-939-2435
HOURS: MON.-FRI. 9 A.M.-5 P.M., SAT. AND SUN. 9 A.M.-6 P.M.;
EXTENDED HOURS THURS. 9 A.M.-10 P.M. (JUNE-AUG.)

JOHN HANCOCK CENTER

Before he bested himself with the Sears Tower, architect Bruce Graham designed the John Hancock Center, erected in 1970 and situated right between busy Michigan Avenue and placid Lake Michigan. The John Hancock Center stands about 300 feet shorter than the United States' tallest building, but it enjoys the status as a beloved Chicago landmark every bit as much as its cousin.

In fact, many visitors actually prefer the Hancock Center to any of Chicago's other skyscrapers. Its placement on the edge of Magnificent Mile makes it an easily accessible and popular meeting point. Its distinctive look recalls the almost skeletal design of the Eiffel Tower (which Graham acknowledged as an influence), boosting its iconic status over the slightly more functional Sears Tower. But its most important attribute of all is a breathtaking view that rivals any other cloud-piercing building in the world.

From the 94th floor observation deck, you can see for miles, and at night the Hancock affords an almost hypnotic view of the airplanes circling over the lake. The open-air Skywalk on the same floor is not for the light-headed. Should the dizzying views prove too much, you can instead concentrate on the timeline of Chicago history and a number of informative kiosks, both of which are certainly less intimidating ways of viewing the city.

If you're craving a meal that's anything but down-to-earth, head to the 95th-floor Signature Room for the popular Sunday brunch or splurge on a pricier dinner, worth it for the view as well as the food. Virtually unique among the world's tallest structures, the John Hancock Center is actually a residential building as well, attracting a number of rich and famous owners. People watchers can make a day of it just waiting at the building's base and admiring the crowded sidewalk.

 B2 875 N. MICHIGAN AVE. 888-875-8439
HOURS: DAILY 9 A.M.-11 P.M.

LINCOLN PARK / LINCOLN PARK ZOO

The abundance of green in Lincoln Park, Chicago's own reserve of open space, belies its city setting. A flurry of North Side activity, Lincoln Park and its numerous attractions draws everyone from athletes in training and lazy sunbathers to museumgoers and animal watchers – a far cry from the park's beginnings as a cemetery for cholera and smallpox victims.

Situated at the heart of Lincoln Park is the Chicago Historical Society, a great place to get a grip on the city and its past. Afterwards, grab an ice cream cone and stroll across the grass to Saint-Gaudens' Lincoln statue, eat at the North Pond, or roam over to the lake to laze in the sun. The relaxing butterfly exhibit awaits at the nearby Peggy Notebaert Nature Museum.

If, all of a sudden, you hear an elephant trumpet interrupt the sound of children playing, don't be alarmed. Lincoln Park is also the home of the popular Lincoln Park Zoo, a sanctuary of animals on display in the middle of an urban jungle. The zoo began in 1868 with a gift of just two swans, but bears, sea lions, and the usual zoo fare were added soon after, some taken in during the Depression when circuses could no longer care for them.

Still free after all these years, the Lincoln Park Zoo also remains committed to research, conservation, and education, offering tours and classes that go beyond exotic imported animals. Anyone with children in tow should check out the Farm-in-the-Zoo, which houses dairy cows, pigs, sheep, horses, and other common creatures. And if you need a break from all the animals, take a relaxing paddleboat trip through the South Lagoon, a safari of solace that perfectly complements a beautiful summer day.

 B4 ZOO: 2200 N. CANNON DR. 312-742-2000
HOURS: DAILY 8 A.M.-6 P.M. (ZOO GROUNDS);
DAILY 10 A.M.-5 P.M. (ZOO BUILDINGS)

MUSEUM OF CONTEMPORARY ART

Chicago's vibrant art scene thrives on the new and alternative and the Museum of Contemporary Art, opened in 1967, is Chicago's monument to this spirit, seeking out the best in modern (post-1945) works for its exhibition halls.

The museum's current building, debuted in 1996 and occupying an enviably central location near the Water Tower, was designed by German architect Josef Paul Kleihues and is itself fittingly contemporary. The cool, modern structure meshes nicely with the diverse multimedia exhibits it typically holds inside. It includes seven times the original exhibition space, allowing the MCA to display several permanent collections alongside a variety of temporary exhibits. Kleihues' design allows bright light to stream in and the resulting views of Lake Michigan may compete with the exhibits for attention. An upscale café on site attracts business lunchers and even has installations hanging from the ceiling.

Featuring the works of such well-known iconoclasts as Cindy Sherman and Andres Serano, both of whom prompted high profile MCA exhibits, as well as more abstract pinnacles of design and artistic daring, the MCA's fare can always be counted on to be challenging, controversial, exciting, and illuminating. It is often the first U.S. museum to give solo shows to groundbreaking artists – it enjoys this distinction with Frida Kahlo and Jeff Koons, among others. The MCA also hosts several one-off events and activities, including the annual Summer Solstice, a 24-hour festival of dance, music, art, film, and performance.

The website (www.mcachicago.org) details current and upcoming exhibits and events, but in many ways an impromptu visit seems the strategy that best suits this museum. Modern art is often about the unexpected, and there is no better way to experience this than to wander in off the street and explore what the MCA has to offer.

 B3 220 E. CHICAGO AVE. 312-280-2660
HOURS: TUES. 10 A.M.-8 P.M., WED.-SUN. 10 A.M.-5 P.M.

MUSEUM OF SCIENCE AND INDUSTRY

 Tucked down in leafy, collegiate Hyde Park, the Museum of Science and Industry has long been one of Chicago's most popular destinations, drawing some two million visitors annually. A virtual playground for adults and children alike, the museum is full of surprises that range from detailed exhibits on genetics to an actual Boeing 727, which made news when it was driven down a closed Lake Shore Drive to its new home.

The MSI, opened in 1933 in the 1893 Columbian Exposition's Palace of Fine Arts building, showcases permanent exhibits that explore the links between science and industry and place them in the context of history or our daily lives. In one of its displays dedicated to farming and coal mining, visitors are taken on a ride that simulates a 600-foot descent into a mine. (The wait for this attraction is *long*.) The challenge posed by AIDS is documented in *The War Within*, a fascinating account of the disease and the fight to cure it. And toeing the line between creepy and cool are actual slices of human bodies prepared in the 1940s. The weak-of-stomach, beware: the display features several preserved cross-section views of male and female cadavers.

Several temporary exhibits make their way to the museum each year and cover the wide variety of topics to be expected at the MSI. They have included 500 timepieces from the collection of Seth G. Atwood (founder of the Time Museum in Rockford, Illinois), a 110-million-year-old, 40-foot-long crocodile skeleton, and a room investigating the roots of rap music and hip-hop culture.

When the time comes to rest your feet, head to the Henry Crown Space Center Omnimax Theater, where the five-story domed theater shows larger-than-life movies (literally). For more terrestrial pleasures, explore the placid Osaka Garden out back, Japan's contribution to the 1893 exposition, where ducks bob in small ponds.

D5 5700 S. LAKE SHORE DR. 773-684-1414 OR 800-468-6674
HOURS: MON.-FRI. 9:30 A.M.-4 P.M., SAT. AND SUN. 9:30 A.M.-5:30 P.M.

NAVY PIER

Redeveloped in the 1990s into a year-round lakeside carnival, Navy Pier takes its place with San Francisco's Fisherman's Wharf and D.C.'s Bureau of Engraving and Printing as Chicago's major destination that locals scorn. Critics complain that it is little more than a waterfront mall, while residents of the adjacent high rises consider the landmark 150-foot-tall Ferris wheel an eyesore. Even so, Navy Pier offers a number of amusements, some cheesy and some unique, that are appreciated by more than eight million visitors each year.

The pier began in 1916 as a successful shipping and recreation hub, but after the University of Illinois, which had occupied the pier since the mid-1940s, left in 1965, it actually sat rusting and unused for much of the late 1970s through early 1990s. Then in 1994, this prime piece of Lake Michigan real estate became the object of a $150 million rehabilitation. Today, unexceptional stores, arcades, and restaurants dominate the pier, but, in addition to some truly wonderful sights, museums, and events, the beautiful views and popular boat tours make the visit worthwhile.

Among the noteworthy attractions, a giant IMAX screen brings several exclusive films to Navy Pier each year and has also been enlisted for popular big screen revivals of various classics and epics. The Chicago Children's Museum offers plenty of diversions for kids, while the acclaimed Chicago Shakespeare Theater serves as a beacon of high culture amongst the fun and games. The Smith Museum of Stained Glass Windows, the only such museum in the United States, opened in 2000.

Along with the pier's permanent exhibitions is seasonal fare such as the annual Flower Show. The Skyline Stage draws dozens of touring bands in the warm months, and when winter arrives, the space converts to an ice-skating rink. During the holidays the Navy Pier structure hosts dozens of parties and New Year festivities, typically topped off by a volley of bright fireworks launched over the lake.

Parking is expensive, though ample, but the city provides a number of convenient free trolley-impersonating buses that leave regularly from various stops downtown.

 D6 600 E. GRAND AVE. 312-595-7437 OR 800-595-7437

PRAIRIE AVENUE HISTORIC DISTRICT

Cities often grow so fast, building over structures considered outdated or obsolete, that what came before can sometimes be forgotten amidst the progress. In Chicago, a pocket of this past has been preserved in the Prairie Avenue Historic District. This area, with its 19th-century mansions and old-time atmosphere, presents a glimpse into what the city was like before it became the massive metropolis it is today.

Most of the buildings along Prairie Avenue date back to the late 1800s. The area survived the 1871 fire to become the neighborhood of choice for the city's rich and powerful – George Pullman and Marshall Field inspired the original housing boom – until the turn of the 20th century when residents started moving north. Many homes were felled as the surrounding neighborhood became increasingly industrial during the first half of the 1900s. However, in the 1960s, preservationists saved the Glessner House and, in the late '70s, the city returned the Clarke House to the area and refashioned it into a museum.

The Greek revival-style Clarke House is the city's oldest building, built in 1836. Nearby is the H. H. Richardson–designed Glessner House, which features an extensive collection of 19th-century decorative arts typical of Chicago's Gilded Age. For something more contemporary, trot across Women's Park to the Woman Made Gallery, a selection of modern art housed in the Keith mansion. Other notables include the Kimball House (1801 S. Prairie Ave.) and the Coleman-Ames House (1811 S. Prairie Ave.), which together are dubbed the Soccer House for their U.S. Soccer Federation occupants.

The rest of the Prairie Avenue neighborhood is currently experiencing a new housing boom, with fresh developments sprouting up every day. The historic homes are, as ever, encircled by modern life, providing a unique and fascinating contrast between old Chicago and new.

 C3 INDIANA AND PRAIRIE AVES. BTWN. 18TH AND CULLERTON STS. 312-326-1480 (TOURS)

SEARS TOWER

Until the Petronas Towers in Kuala Lumpur, Malaysia, controversially usurped its title, the Sears Tower stood as the tallest building in the world. But whether or not the skyscraper remains the world's tallest building or merely the world's tallest occupied building – a subtle distinction made by the Council on Tall Buildings and Urban Habitat after several complaints – there's no question that the Sears Tower is the reigning champion of the Chicago skyline.

Designed by Bruce Graham and erected in 1973, the Sears Tower scratches the stratosphere with its awe-inspiring 1,454 feet. It is so tall that on certain days the weather at the 110th floor is different than the weather on the ground. Staring up at the structure simply does not do it justice. Rather, everyone save the severely acrophobic needs to ascend to the Skydeck on one of the fast elevators, which nonetheless seem to take forever. Once your ears have popped and the doors open on the top floor, the long lines and vertiginous climb both seem worth it.

The top floor of the tower is a privileged perch worth savoring. On a clear day the observation deck allows you to peer over 50 miles of land, taking in all of Chicago's other, suddenly small-looking buildings, much of the massive Lake Michigan, and sometimes parts of other states. City planning never looks as impressive as it does from this bird's-eye view, where the logic of the Chicago's layout is laid bare. From the top of the Sears Tower you can study Chicago's neatly criss-crossing grid, following the streets to sights you have already seen or sneaking a glance at future destinations, often little more than tiny specks from this point nearly a third of a mile straight up. Or, take this opportunity to spy on all of the rooftop swimming pools, otherwise invisible from the ground.

 C5 233 S. WACKER DR. 312-875-9696
HOURS: DAILY 10 A.M.-10 P.M. (MAY-SEPT.); DAILY 10 A.M.-8 P.M. (OCT.-APR.)

UNIVERSITY OF CHICAGO/ROBIE HOUSE

Incorporated in 1890, the University of Chicago has been the site of many intellectual benchmarks and historic moments. This academic powerhouse has racked up more Nobel Prizes than any other school, and its campus, for better or for worse, witnessed the world's first controlled nuclear reaction.

Known more for its students and faculty's mental, rather than physical, achievements, the university nonetheless can always claim to have educated the first Heisman Trophy winner. However, the school's days of athletic dominance are long gone. The football field was replaced by the Regenstein Library, and even former University president Robert Maynard Hutchins once famously quipped, "Whenever I feel like exercising, I lie down until the feeling passes."

Aside from supplying its city home with college graduates for the work force, the university sustains a thriving cultural scene in its Hyde Park neighborhood. The University of Chicago's Smart Museum of Art, Oriental Institute, and the Renaissance Society display intriguing works that span the globe and human history. The Court Theatre is a world-class playhouse, belying the school's reputation as the birthplace of improvised comedy, and the Documentary Film Group, one of the country's most respected student film organizations, screens everything from big-budget blockbusters to esoteric art films in the well-funded Max Palevsky Theater.

Visitors to the university can take in some of these cultural offerings, or stroll the centenarian campus to check out its Gothic architecture. The towering Rockefeller Chapel, with its ever-ringing carillon bells, is perhaps the best example of the school's architectural style.

A departure from the dominant medievalesque structures, Frank Lloyd Wright's Robie House is one of the campus's most popular attractions. Wright considered the 1909 Prairie style-home to be the "the cornerstone of modern architecture," and decades later it remains just as fresh. More than 170 ornate doors and windows help give the Robie House its open, airy feel, and by taking the guided tour you can get a closer, informed look at how Wright achieved such a feat.

 D3 5801 S. ELLIS AVE. 773-702-1234

WATER TOWER

So many of Chicago's landmarks can be traced back to just after 1871, the year the Great Fire forced the city to rebuild itself virtually from scratch. The Water Tower, on the other hand, is one of the few prominent landmarks that predates the fire, since it was the only public structure to survive the blaze. Although nowhere near as impressive as many of Chicago's grander sights, this historic presence serves as a constant reminder of where Chicago's roots lie and is a testament to Midwestern tenacity.

William W. Boyington's limestone tower was built in the Windy City in 1869, just two years before fate would transform it into an instant icon. The 154-foot tall fortresslike structure was designed in the anachronistic castellated Gothic style. Compared to the skyscrapers that surround it, the building is beyond modest, overshadowed by modern constructions and bustling shopping centers, but its central location, right on Magnificant Mile, amplifies its symbolism.

No longer housing the standpipe it was originally built to hide, the Water Tower currently displays local art and is the home of the city's official photo gallery. Its sister entity, the old Pumping Station, sits across Michigan Avenue and houses a simple visitor center where you can take a behind-the-scenes look at Chicago's waterworks.

3 **B2** 806 N. MICHIGAN AVE. 312-742-0808
HOURS: MON.–SAT. 10 A.M.–6:30 P.M., SUN. 10 A.M.–5 P.M.

SIDE WALKS

• Shop Chiasso and the rest of Water Tower Place for anything
B2 835 N. MICHIGAN AVE. 312-280-1249
• Join journalists and politicians over a burger at Billy Goat Tavern
D2 430 N. MICHIGAN AVE. 312-222-1525
• See the sights from a horse-drawn carriage
B2 820 N. MICHIGAN AVE. 312-266-7878
• Martinis at the Coq d'Or inside the Drake
A2 140 E. WALTON PLACE 312-787-2200

WRIGLEY FIELD

With its familiar red sign proclaiming this the "Home of Chicago Cubs," Wrigley Field is Chicago team spirit enshrined. Nevermind that the Cubs haven't won the World Series since 1908, the longest drought in baseball history, the faithful continue to flock here and Cubs games consistently sell out.

Built in 1914, the second oldest major league ballpark in the country (Boston's 1912 Fenway is the oldest) has a surprisingly unified history. The stadium first welcomed the Cubs in 1916 and the two have been synonymous ever since.

The nine-inning party known as game day attracts hundreds of families, visitors, and bleacher bums to drink beer, inhale hot dogs, and perhaps even cheer on the team. The experience is hardly confined to the park itself. Bars in the neighborhood (some of which have bleachers on their roofs) reach capacity well before the first pitch and hopefuls congregate alongside the ballpark walls, waiting for an errant home-run ball to clear the stadium.

A planned redesign might sacrifice some of the stadium's flavor in favor of better sight lines and more seating, but nothing can dampen the sense of nostalgia that surrounds Wrigley Field. Visitors, prepare to catch a bit of the infectious spirit, whether on a ballpark tour or with coveted tickets in hand.

 B3 1060 W. ADDISON ST. 773-404-2827, 800-843-2827 (TICKETS)
HOURS: CALL FOR TOUR TIMES

SIDE WALKS

- Stroll Alta Vista Terrace
  A2 START AT N. ALTA VISTA TER. AND GRACE ST.
- Trove Flashy Trash for vintage costumes
  B3 3524 N. HALSTED ST. 773-327-6900
- Ann Sather restaurant for pre-game Swedish meatballs
  C3 929 W. BELMONT AVE. 773-348-2378
- Raise a glass for the team at Murphy's Bleachers
  B3 3655 N. SHEFFIELD AVE. 773-281-5356

® **RESTAURANTS**

DIRECTORY OF RESTAURANTS

HOT SPOTS

QUICK BITES

ROMANTIC

ADOBO GRILL

Exposed brick, earth tones, and Diego Rivera–inspired paintings lend a festive yet sophisticated air to this casa of haute Mexican cuisine. The margaritas come in martini glasses and servers whip up the guacamole at your table. Tequila lovers, be prepared to make some tough choices. $$

 D4 1610 N. WELLS ST.
312-266-7999

ANN SATHER

This cozy mainstay has some of the best Scandinavian food this side of Stockholm. The fresh-baked cinnamon rolls are dangerously addictive and fans line up to get their fix on

 weekend mornings. For a savory alternative, try the Swedish meatballs at lunch or dinner. $

 C3 929 W. BELMONT AVE.
773-348-2378

ATHENA GREEK RESTAURANT

One of the classier Greektown spots, Athena livens up its spacious dining room with murals of a Grecian village and waiters shouting "Opa!" while holding flaming dishes of *saganaki*. If you prefer your kebabs alfresco, sit in the massive outdoor patio. $$

 C2 212 S. HALSTED ST.
312-655-0000

THE BAGEL RESTAURANT & DELI

The crowd tends to skew older at this New York deli look-alike. Folks line the long lunch counter to fill up on giant matzo balls, heaping Reubens, and the homemaker's cure-all, chicken noodle soup. Posters from old musicals cheer up the otherwise generic surroundings. $

 D4 3107 N. BROADWAY ST.
773-477-0300

THE BERGHOFF

It's always Oktoberfest in this merry old-world landmark that brims with stained glass and dark wood. Laying claim to Chicago's first liquor license, the Berghoff serves up homemade root beer and bourbon along with its requisite German fare. $$

 B6 17 W. ADAMS ST.
312-427-3170

BILLY GOAT TAVERN

 The greasy food takes a backseat to the Goat's legendary down-and-dirty atmosphere. Journalists, politicians, and blue-collar joes swap stories over burgers and beer in this basement dive. Cooks will oblige if you'd like to hear John Belushi's "cheezborger cheezborger" line, but unlike the skit, it's no Pepsi, Coke. $

 D2 430 N. MICHIGAN AVE.
312-222-1525

BISTROT MARGOT

Dark wood, burgundy banquettes, and black-and-white tiled floors add to the French bistro feel of this affordable hot spot, where the food is as authentic as the ambiance. Try the *steak au poivre,* a generous New York strip with black peppercorns and crispy frites. $$

 E4 1437 N. WELLS ST.
312-587-3660

BONGO ROOM

Tiny airplane propellers double as ceiling fans at this cozy-but-cool eatery that offers breakfast – and lunch – until 2:30 P.M. Those who blur the line between breakfast and dessert can indulge in the chocolate tower French toast during the wildly popular weekend brunch. $

 D3 1470 N. MILWAUKEE AVE.
773-489-0690

CAFE BA-BA-REEBA!

 Fun-loving, attractive singles have to eat and this is where they do it. Large groups pass pitchers of sangria and tiny plates of tapas in this cavernous restaurant, where the colorful décor and cacophony of voices are equally loud. $$

 B1 2024 N. HALSTED ST.
773-935-5000

CAFE IBERICO

Even though this tapas bar is about the size of Spain, it never seems to have enough tables for the throngs who come for the cheap-yet-tasty array of traditional dishes. It gets noisy at this high-energy eatery, especially after the drinks have been flowing for a few hours. $

 C5 739 N. LASALLE ST.
312-573-1510

CALYPSO CAFE

Calpyso Cafe takes its Caribbean theme from the menu – jerk chicken and conch dishes – to the atmosphere and décor – steel drum music, tropical plants, brightly colored cushions. Be prepared to compete with local families for a seat at the Sunday brunch. $$

 C4 5211 S. HARPER AVE.
773-955-0229

CARSON'S BBQ RIBS, STEAKS & CHOPS

Conventioneers congregate in this Chicago institution, where the walls are plastered with autographed photos of the athletes, newscasters, and entertainers that have savored Carson's legendary ribs. The chewy baby backs are smoked with natural hickory. $$

 C5 612 N. WELLS ST.
312-280-9200

▲

CEDARS OF LEBANON

The tasty food offerings at this Middle Eastern eatery make up for its less than authentic surroundings. Try the heaping plate of hummus with pita bread or the falafel. $

 B4 1618 E. 53RD ST.
773-324-6227

CHARLIE TROTTER'S

A conservative, moneyed clientele comes for the top-notch service and superlative cuisine at this world-famous restaurant. Trotter's is the restaurant award darling of Chicago, so book months in advance and leave yourself lots of time to work through the fixed-price meals, a melange of American, French, and Asian influences. $$$

 B1 816 W. ARMITAGE AVE.
773-248-6228

CHICAGO FIREHOUSE

Housed in an early 1900s fire station, this bastion of fine dining is a favorite lunch spot with politicos who broker big deals over even bigger steaks. No hokey red helmets or hoses here – just a few tasteful brass fire poles remain. $$$

 A3 1401 S. MICHIGAN AVE.
312-786-1401

CHICAGO FLAT SAMMIES

Michigan Avenue shoppers in need of a quick, caloric pick-me-up file in for the flat bread pizzas, creative "sammiches," and generous salads. Eat inside in the historic Pumping Station, or people watch from the sidewalk cafe. $

 B2 811 N. MICHIGAN AVE.
312-664-2733

CHICAGO PIZZA & OVEN GRINDER

Across from the site of the notorious St. Valentine's Day Massacre sits this cozy, cabinlike restaurant that packs in a happy-go-lucky crowd of regulars. Die-hard fans wax poetic about the pizza potpie, gigantic oven grinders (slightly oven-baked submarine sandwiches), and Mediterranean bread appetizer. $

 B3 2121 N. CLARK ST.
773-248-2570

CLUB LUCKY

This swanky diner dishes up the city's best eggplant parmigiana. Enjoy it with a blue-cheese olive martini in one of their comfy red booths. After you're done, take a bit of this beloved Italian restaurant home in a jar of their marinara sauce. $$

 D3 1824 W. WABANSIA AVE.
773-227-2300

CROFTON ON WELLS

The spartan candlelit dining room at this River North restaurant provides an intimate setting for Suzy Crofton's innovative contemporary American cuisine. The seasonally changing menu showcases elegant, restrained dishes and the cordial servers know how to pick the right wine to go with them. $$$

 D5 535 N. WELLS ST. 312-755-1790

DIXIE KITCHEN & BAIT SHOP

A garageful of antiques clutter this laid-back, family-friendly joint that resembles a backwater shack south of the Mason-Dixon line. The kitchen serves up tasty jambalaya, gumbo, po'boys, and other Cajun classics every day, starting at 11 A.M. $

 B4 5225 S. HARPER AVE. 773-363-4943

EARWAX

The slightly disgusting name – a remnant of the coffeehouse's previous incarnation as a record store – belies the tasty food at this popular spot. An amiable slacker-type wait staff sells vegetarian-friendly food in front and videos in back. The 1940s vintage circus banners add to the carnivalesque atmosphere. $

 D2 1564 N. MILWAUKEE AVE. 773-772-4019

ED DEBEVIC'S

When they're not taking orders or bringing out burgers, 'dogs, and milk shakes, the sassy, gum-snapping servers dance on the counters of this '50s-style diner. Route 66 road signs and other Americana blanket the walls and can provide a distraction during the sometimes outrageously long wait. $

 C5 640 N. WELLS ST. 312-664-1707

EPITOME

A true pioneer in this restaurant-starved area of the Loop, Epitome is a green marble lair, with live jazz on weekends, where casually elegant couples treat one another to crab cakes and champagne. After dinner, many head to the upstairs nightclub. $$$

 E3 2347 S. MICHIGAN AVE. 312-326-2300

EVEREST

This restaurant's Himalayan prices are worth it for the tuxedoed waiters, 40th-floor view, and chef Jean Joho's French food, the best in the city. Embrace the extravagance and order the carnaroli risotto, which comes topped with (edible) 24-karat gold leaf. $$$

 C5 440 S. LASALLE ST. 312-663-8920

GEJA'S CAFE

Most Chicago couples have been to this dimly lit, subterranean restaurant on at least one special date. The nightly flamenco guitarist and the intimacy of the fondue-centered food make Geja's a favorite for romantic dining. $$$

 B3 340 W. ARMITAGE AVE. 773-281-9101

GENE & GEORGETTI

For more than 60 years, alto-voiced waiters have been doling out shoe-sized T-bones at Gene & Georgetti, the oldest steakhouse in a city of steakhouses. This den was a favorite of Frank Sinatra's and its institutional status is confirmed by its role in the HBO series *Mind of the Married Man.* $$$

 D5 500 N. FRANKLIN ST. 312-527-3718

GIBSONS STEAKHOUSE

This white-hot steakhouse is a meat market, from the sizzling slabs of steak to the swinging singles who come to feast and flirt. Photos of celebs are plastered on the wooden walls of the clubby joint and people watching is a favorite pastime. $$$

 A1 1028 N. RUSH ST. 312-266-8999

GINO'S EAST

Housed in the gargantuan former

Planet Hollywood, Gino's East is the only place in the city where graffiti is not only allowed, it's encouraged. Leave your mark, then savor the famed deep-dish pizza with the trademark buttery crust. $

 C5 633 N. WELLS ST.
312-988-4200

GIOCO

The dim lights, brick walls, and desolate location give Gioco a slightly illicit air and recall its past as a Prohibition-era speakeasy. The pricey Italian wine list pairs nicely with rustic fare from the same region. For ultimate privacy, sit in the old safe. $$

 A3 1312 S. WABASH AVE.
312-939-3870

GOLDEN APPLE

The door's never locked at this 24-hour diner featured in an episode of public radio's *This American Life*. It draws a varied clientele of cops, couples, and hungry bar hoppers with a hankering for bacon and eggs long after the sun goes down. $

 D1 2971 N. LINCOLN AVE.
773-528-1413

GOURMAND

 Grab one of the free alternative newspapers and join the college students and young bohemians who delight in Gourmand's ever-flowing coffee, fresh-baked muffins, and gourmet sandwiches. Abstract art and blackboard menus hang from the goldenrod walls in this hip, loftlike cafe. $

 D6 728 S. DEARBORN ST.
312-427-2610

GREEN DOLPHIN STREET

This swanky supper club abutting the river serves a regularly changing menu of contemporary American cuisine and caters mostly to Jay Gatsby-types of a certain age, whose musical tastes are in synch with the live jazz offerings. $$$

 B4 2200 N. ASHLAND AVE.
773-395-0066

HACKNEY'S

Situated in the oldest building in historic Printer's Row, Hackney's has been making its celebrated burgers the same way since 1939: a thick disc of ground beef flanked by fresh-baked dark rye. The service is friendly and an all-ages crowd frequents this cozy loft. $

 D6 733 S. DEARBORN ST.
312-461-1116

HALF SHELL

In this dark sublevel hang-out, seafood aficionados can dig into succulent Alaskan king crab legs at the Formica tables or pull up to the bar and watch the Bears, Bulls, or Cubs on TV. $$

 E4 676 W. DIVERSEY PKWY.
773-549-1773

HARRY CARAY'S

 Just like the lovable late Chicago Cubs announcer it's named after, Harry Caray's is a Chicago institution. Grab a beer at the always-crowded bar, then head into the surprisingly elegant dining room for chicken vesuvio, hailed as the best by the Chicago Tribune. $$$

 D6 33 W. KINZIE ST.
312-828-0966

HEAT

The specialties at this tiny, elegant restaurant are not for the queasy: the freshly killed fish is often still twitching on the plate. For the less adventurous, there are more standard, though still top-notch, sushi options. On weekends, a deejay raises the usual buzz to a trendy pulse. $$$

 E3 1507 N. SEDGWICK ST.
312-397-9818

HONG MIN

Those in search of cool surroundings and friendly service, keep looking. But if you're craving cheap and delicious Chinese food – especially seafood – park yourself in one of the chintzy chairs and thumb through the massive menu of this Chinatown mainstay. $

 D1 221 W. CERMAK RD.
312-842-5026

ITALIAN VILLAGE

Offering more dining options than some real Italian villages, this three-restaurant complex has something for everyone. Couples wanting a romantic, fine-dining experience should head to Vivere; families favor The Village for traditional Northern Italian cuisine; and the cozy La Cantina specializes in seafood. **$$**

 B1 71 W. MONROE ST.
312-332-7005

JACKSON HARBOR GRILL

This former park district boathouse has evolved into one of the best alfresco restaurants in the city. Only open during spring and summer, the shorefront Jackson Harbor Grill offers a spicy selection of everything from rib eye to sea scallops. **$$**

 F6 6401 S. COAST GUARD DR.
773-288-4442

KAMEHACHI

It's a wasabi-hot hipster scene in this sushi restaurant's dimly lit upstairs café. For a little fresh air, eat your Chicago Crazy Rolls, a heaping mouthful of yellowtail, tuna, salmon, crab, cucumbers, and *masago*, in the picturesque outdoor garden. Neophytes will appreciate the selection of all-cooked sushi. **$$**

 E4 1400 N. WELLS ST.
312-664-3663

KLAY OVEN

Some of the Japanese ambience still lingers in this former sushi restaurant, but the food is straight up Indian, prepared in the tandoor – or clay oven – style. If the soothing atmosphere isn't enough to help you unwind, a few Indian beers should do the trick. **$$**

 D4 414 N. ORLEANS ST.
312-527-3999

LA PASADITA

You're not seeing triple: Three La Pasaditas sit within a few steps of each other to serve the masses who flock to these holes-in-the-wall for delicious steak burritos and tongue tacos, which taste better than they sound. **$**

 F4 1132 N. ASHLAND AVE.
773-384-6537

▲

LA PETITE FOLIE

The quaint La Petite Folie means Hyde Park intellectuals no longer have to schlep up to the North Side for escargot and other gourmet specialties. The pleasant servers double as sommeliers and are happy to help you choose a French wine to wash down your fromage. **$$**

 C4 1504 E. 55TH ST.
773-493-1394

LE BOUCHON

Flower boxes and café curtains adorn the front windows of this charming storefront, where indirect lighting and crisp white tablecloths make even a casual supper seem special. Bentwood chairs are occupied by cute couples relishing the reasonably priced Lyonese food. **$$**

 B2 1958 N. DAMEN AVE.
773-862-6600

LE COLONIAL

This upscale French-influenced Vietnamese eatery draws a mix of DKNY-wearing club kids and middle-aged Gold Coasters with menu items like the crisp-seared whole red snapper in spicy-sour sauce. Upstairs, pull up a wicker chair and lounge under lazy ceiling fans. **$$**

 A1 937 N. RUSH ST.
312-255-0088

LES NOMADES

Jacket and tie are the dress code at acclaimed chef/owner Roland Liccioni's newest French restaurant. Miro originals and fresh flowers adorn the stately, four-star eatery and you'll have no problem finding a wine to go with the refined four-course fixed-price menu. **$$$**

 C2 222 E. ONTARIO ST.
312-649-9010

LOU MITCHELL'S

Dine-n-dash power brokers come for the huge skillet breakfasts heaping with eggs, bacon, and potatoes. Old-school waitresses are quick with the coffee, and the beige booths and plastic plants provide a comforting, although somewhat dated, atmosphere. $

 C3 565 W. JACKSON BLVD.
312-939-3111

MAGGIANO'S LITTLE ITALY

 Fast for a week before coming to this bastion of big portions. The red-and-white checkered tablecloths and vintage photographs give an air of Italian-home-cooking authenticity to this chain restaurant where the adept servers can be relentlessly cheerful and the noise level becomes boisterous at peak times. $$

 D6 516 N. CLARK AVE.
312-644-7700

MANNY'S COFFEE SHOP AND DELI

What Manny's lacks in atmosphere, it makes up in quantity. Monstrous servings of corned beef, pastrami, and other deli faves get dished up cafeteria style in this South Side institution. Open for breakfast and lunch. $

 F3 1141 S. JEFFERSON ST.
312-939-2855

MARCHÉ

With its Moulin Rouge décor, thumping club music, and a wait staff fresh off the catwalk, Marché deserves all the buzz surrounding it. The French fare is prepared with a twist, with dishes like the duck duet accompanied by purple mashed potatoes. $$$

 F2 833 W. RANDOLPH ST.
312-226-8399

MAS/OTRO MAS

Pretty people huddle around the bar sipping creative cocktails as they wait for a table at this Latin American hot spot renowned for its daily ceviche. The main Wicker Park location is dinner only, but its smaller sister restaurant, Otro Mas, is open for Sunday brunch. $$

 F3 1670 W. DIVISION ST.
773-276-8700

 B1 3651 N. SOUTHPORT AVE.
773-348-3200

MAZA

Want a crash course in Lebanese food? Order the maza deluxe appetizer and the more than a dozen tiny plates of scintillating hors d'oeuvres will educate you with stuffed grape leaves, spicy lamb sausage, and tabouleh salad. $$

 E2 2748 N. LINCOLN AVE.
773-929-9600

MEDICI

University of Chicago students poring over textbooks and feeding on lamb ragout are typical in the Med, where coffee- and pizza-guzzling gargoyles guard the front entrance. Squeeze your own orange juice and peruse the countless names etched into the wooden tables. $

 D3 1327 E. 57TH ST.
773-667-7394

MIA FRANCESCA

Two-hour waits for a spot in the noisy, narrow dining room are not unusual at this bustling North Side Italian restaurant. Handsomely decorated, this popular date destination offers bountiful plates of pasta and thin-crust pizzas, which are perfect for sharing. $$

 C3 3311 N. CLARK ST.
773-281-3310

MIKE DITKA'S RESTAURANT

The gruff former Chicago Bears coach drops in his namesake eatery a few times a week. Da coach's signature dish? "Da Pork Chop," of course. Don't be fooled by the abundant sports memorabilia: This is higher-end dining with prices to match. $$$

 B2 100 E. CHESTNUT ST.
312-587-8989

MK

The patrons here are as reservedly fashionable as the décor, which features exposed brick walls and a massive skylight. The food from acclaimed chef Michael Kornick is the standout – the venison earns raves as does the banana dessert. $$$

 B5 868 N. FRANKLIN ST.
312-482-9179

MOD

You'll find the hipster set in MOD's spartan digs, which serve as an ultramodern backdrop for the contemporary American menu built around artisanal ingredients, like Spanish sheep's milk cheese and hand-ground grits from North Carolina. Expect cotton candy with your check, but don't expect a quiet dinner. $$

 D2 1520 N. DAMEN AVE. 773-252-1500

MR. BEEF

On Mr. Beef's communal picnic bench, truck drivers literally rub elbows with power brokers and celebs (Jay Leno is a regular). All are lured to this humble hole-in-the-wall by the messy, peppery, garlicky Italian beef sandwiches. $

 C4 666 N. ORLEANS ST. 312-337-8500

NAHA

Sleek walnut floors and a slightly Asian ambience combine to create a calm, yet sexy, atmosphere at Naha, the much-hyped home of former Four Seasons Beverly Hills chef Carrie Nahabedian. Her contemporary American cuisine shows Mediterranean influences, like in the Greek salad served with a feta cheese turnover. $$$

 D6 500 N. CLARK ST. 312-321-6242

NICK'S FISHMARKET

A frequent line item on expense accounts, Nick's Fishmarket exudes a simple elegance that's appropriate whether you're trying to land a deal or pop the question. The color scheme may be earthy, but the food is emphatically aquatic. $$$

B6 51 S. CLARK ST. 312-621-0200

NINE

Cleavage and caviar abound in this sensual steak-and-seafood outpost, where the good food is secondary to the attractive see-and-be-seen crowd. Don't leave without trying a glow-in-the-dark Midori martini in the très chic upstairs Ghost Bar. $$$

 A4 440 W. RANDOLPH ST. 312-575-9900

NOMI

Choose from more than 6,000 bottles of wine to complement chef Sandro Gamba's award-winning haute cuisine. Try the halibut while enjoying the restaurant's spectacular view. During the warm weather months, the outdoor terrace of NoMI Garden opens for cocktails, sushi, and brochette. $$$

 B2 800 N. MICHIGAN AVE. 312-239-4030

NORTH POND

 This former ice skaters' shelter has been transformed into an idyllic dining spot nestled in the heart of Lincoln Park. The Prairie-style décor lends a cozy air to this high-end eatery and the seasonally changing menu emphasizes local organic ingredients. $$$

 F5 2610 N. CANNON DR. 773-477-5845

THE ORIGINAL PANCAKE HOUSE

This popular, cramped eatery boasts 20 varieties of pancakes, from chocolate chip to pineapple-laden Hawaiian. Try the massive apple version, slathered in rich butter and brown sugar. Come before 8 A.M. on weekends to avoid lines that can stretch down the block. $

 A1 22 E. BELLEVUE PLACE 312-642-7917

PEGASUS

 Tasty Mediterranean tapas and entrées are served year-round in this Greektown institution, but the best time to visit is summer, when the rooftop deck is open. The outdoor menu is abbreviated, but it's a worthwhile tradeoff for phenomenal views of the city's skyscrapers. $$

 B2 130 S. HALSTED ST.
312-226-3377

PENNY'S NOODLE SHOP

 Penny knows noodles. This first and smallest of Penny's three locations is packed with locals filling up on *pad thai* and mouth-watering *gyoza* dumplings. This pan-Asian place gets so noisy, you might not even notice the El trains roaring overhead. $

 C3 340 N. SHEFFIELD AVE.
773-281-8222

PICK ME UP CAFE

 If you need a legal concoction sure to keep you up all night, this is your place. The friendly staff pours potent cups of caffeine 24 hours a day on weekends and until 3 A.M. the rest of the week, making Pick Me Up a haven for hip night owls. $

 C3 3408 N. CLARK ST.
773-248-6613

PIECE

Offering an alternative to the Chicago deep dish, this sprawling, airy joint produces pizza with a thin crust that is a delicious but contradictory blend of soft and crunchy. This garage-turned-restaurant was a hit with the cast of MTV's *Real World Chicago,* filmed across the street. $

 D2 1927 W. NORTH AVE.
773-772-4422

PIZZERIA UNO

Try Chicago's famed deep-dish pizza at the place that invented it back in 1943. The gooey, savory pie makes it worth the probable wait. If hunger pangs outweigh your patience, head one block north to Uno's more spacious sister restaurant, Pizzeria Due. $

 D1 29 E. OHIO ST.
312-321-1000

PRAIRIE

South Loop professionals and theater fans mingle in this Frank Lloyd Wright-inspired space. The regional menu relies heavily on Midwestern ingredients like Michigan mushrooms and berries, Illinois-made

feta, and Indiana-grown duck. $$$

 D6 500 S. DEARBORN ST.
312-663-1143

PRINTER'S ROW

A meticulously restored vintage 20th-century building sets a genteel stage for theatergoers wanting to round out their evening with a meal that's sure to satisfy. Noted for its game dishes, the contemporary American menu changes with the seasons. $$$

 D6 550 S. DEARBORN ST.
312-461-0780

PUMP ROOM

Booth No. 1 in the legendary Pump Room was once an obligatory stop on the '50s celebrity circuit. Though the clientele is no longer star studded, it remains a Chicago institution and serves breakfast and glamorous dinners that can start with the brioche toast-accompanied caviar sampler. $$$

 E5 1301 N. STATE PKWY.
312-266-0360

RHAPSODY

Floor-to-ceiling windows overlook a small urban garden in this elegant, highly acclaimed eatery popular with Chicago Symphony ticket-holders. Carpet and soundproofing mean patrons have no problem carrying on a conversation over their American-French meals. $$$

 B2 65 E. ADAMS ST.
312-786-9911

ROCK 'N ROLL MCDONALD'S

 The busiest McDonald's in the United States, this branch of the ubiquitous fast-food chain is filled with hundreds of pieces of rock memorabilia, including a guitar signed by Chuck Berry, life-size plaster casts of the Beatles, and an authentic 1959 Corvette. $

 C6 600 N. CLARK ST.
312-664-7940

ROSEANGELIS

Filled with thirtysomethings dressed in Banana Republic, this imminently popular Italian eatery serves a largely vegetarian menu. Several small, intimate rooms and the casual wait

39

staff make this place feel just like home. $$

 F2 1314 W. WRIGHTWOOD AVE.
773-296-0081

RUSSIAN TEA TIME

 Though the service can be hit or miss, this landmark restaurant always churns out authentic Soviet sustenance to pre-symphony or post-Art Institute diners. Burgundy tablecloths play host to vodka flights, caviar, blinis, and, of course, tea. $$

 B2 77 E. ADAMS ST.
312-360-0000

¡SALPICÓN!

Chef/owner Priscila Satkoff whips up variations on her Mexican grandmother's recipes in this upscale storefront restaurant. Order a tasting flight to sample some top-shelf tequila. The colorful décor is, in a word, bright. $$$

 F4 1252 N. WELLS ST.
312-988-7811

SEASONS

Seasons only uses regional ingredients from local producers to create its four-star, contemporary American menu. The stately private dining rooms are often booked for business dinners, while well-dressed couples wine and dine in the equally attractive main area. $$$

 B2 120 E. DELAWARE PLACE
312-649-2349

SHANGHAI TERRACE

 The Peninsula Hotel's homage to a 1930s Shanghai supper club features wok-fried lobster and five-spiced duck in an intimate 55-seat setting. When weather permits, diners spill out onto the actual terrace, one of the city's most spectacular outdoor patios. $$$

 C2 108 E. SUPERIOR ST.
312-573-6744

SHAW'S CRAB HOUSE

Reminiscent of an old New England seafood house, this restaurant pulls in locals and tourists alike with some of the freshest fish in town. For a more casual experience that's more budget-friendly, head next door to Shaw's New Orleans-inspired Blue Crab Lounge. $$$

 D1 21 E. HUBBARD ST.
312-527-2722

SIGNATURE ROOM AT THE 95TH

Perched atop the John Hancock Center, this first-rate restaurant serves standard American fare – the specialty is roasted rack of lamb – at prices to match its location. If you're without a reservation in the art deco dining room, arrive early and request a window seat on the south side. $$$

 B2 875 N. MICHIGAN AVE.
312-787-9596

SOUL KITCHEN

Located in the hub of the trendy Bucktown/Wicker Park area, Soul Kitchen proudly proclaims itself to be the home of loud food and spicy music. Funky Southern-style fare is served amid high black banquettes and leopard-spotted columns. Weekends welcome the "Soul brunch." $$

 D2 1576 N. MILWAUKEE AVE.
773-342-9742

SPIAGGIA

 Socialites and celebrities take a seat for Tony Mantuano's culinary creations at Chicago's only four-star Italian restaurant. Spiaggia's tables also offer an unparalleled view of Michigan Avenue, but if you can't get one, the adjacent café is an excellent alternative. $$$

 A2 980 N. MICHIGAN AVE.
312-280-2750

SPRING

This bathhouse-turned-restaurant has made quite a splash on the city's dining scene. The adventurous seafood- and vegetable-dominated menu are touched by Asian influences that also show up in the surroundings – a Zen garden precedes the serene dining room. $$$

 D2 2039 W. NORTH AVE.
773-395-7100

SQUARE ONE

Cigarette- and alcohol-free, this squeaky sleek café entertains its cool kid population with magazines, movies, and deejays and nourishes them with juice bar concoctions and munchies like sweet 'n' spicy calamari. On weekends, the kitchen closes at 4 A.M. $

 D2 1561 N. MILWAUKEE AVE.
773-227-7111

STANDING ROOM ONLY

The testosterone-heavy crowd – including nearby resident Mayor Daley – can't get enough of SRO's turkey burgers. A good bet for a fast lunch, this deli-style joint is long on sports posters and pennants and short on tables and chairs. $

 D6 610 S. DEARBORN ST.
312-360-1776

SUSHI WABI

Hipsters and loud music, deejay-spun on weekends, make for a lively scene in the austere setting – small metal chairs, industrial wood block tables, exposed steel supports – of Sushi Wabi. The service can be slow, but the sushi never disappoints. $$

 F2 842 W. RANDOLPH ST.
312-563-1224

TEMPO CAFE

This cozy corner spot really hits its stride on the weekends, when families, old folks, and young singles keep the cash register ringing non-stop until midafternoon. Omelet lovers have a choice of more than 25 variations, all served in a skillet. $

 B1 6 E. CHESTNUT ST.
312-943-4373

THREE HAPPINESS

Ironically, there are only two Three Happiness restaurants. The tiny original location sits in the shadow of this mammoth, two-story restaurant decked out with gaudy dragon prints and other Chinese kitsch. The dim sum brunch served every day until 3 P.M. is among the best in town. $

 D1 2130 S. WENTWORTH AVE.
312-791-1228

▲

TIZI MELLOUL

At this exotic Mediterranean restaurant, diners have a choice of the communal dining room, where they can sit on the floor at knee-high copper tables, or the more conventional main area. On Sundays, belly dancers perform in the shared space. $$

 D5 531 N. WELLS ST.
312-670-4338

TOAST

Soccer moms and dads show off their adorable babies in this comfortable, gourmet breakfast and lunch spot. Thai chicken-spinach tortilla wraps and French toast loaded with strawberries bring in crowds, especially on weekends. $

 B2 746 W. WEBSTER AVE.
773-935-5600

 B2 2046 N. DAMEN AVE.
773-772-5600

TOPOLOBAMPO

Chicago's most esteemed Mexican restaurant sizzles thanks to celebrity chef Rick Bayless's authentic fare. It's easier to snag a table at the adjacent, more casual Frontera Grill. Both restaurants serve stellar margaritas and decorate with colorful Mexican art. $$$

 D6 445 N. CLARK ST.
312-661-1434

TRATTORIA NO. 10

Arches and pillars divide the sprawling subterranean dining room into intimate alcoves. This favorite theatergoer haunt boasts a lengthy Italian menu and a popular early evening weeknight buffet. $$

 B6 10 N. DEARBORN ST.
312-984-1718

TRU

 With its dining room Warhol and arty four-star meals, Tru is modern in food and atmosphere. Flawless service, caviar on tiny glass staircases, and Gale Gand's inimitable desserts keep the upscale clientele booking tables months in advance. $$$

 C2 676 N. ST. CLAIR ST.
312-202-0001

TWIN ANCHORS

Most joints famous for ribs don't have a maritime theme, but the venerable Twin Anchors is the exception. Seafood is on the menu, but don't bother. Carnivores flock here for fall-off-the-bone baby backs dripping with a tomato-based sauce. $$

 D3 1655 N. SEDGWICK ST.
312-266-1616

UNCOMMON GROUND

 The grad school set lingers over bowls of foaming cappuccino in this ideal warming-up spot, but when the sun's out, the crowds migrate to sidewalk tables. This café also hosts surprisingly good live music on most nights of the week. $$

 A2 1214 W. GRACE ST.
773-929-3680

VALOIS

Valois' surly servers dish up comfort food cafeteria style. This Hyde Park institution, immortalized in Mitchell Duneier's novel *Slim's Table,* has the dubious distinction of being among the top greasy spoons in the city. It's certainly the only one with fluffy clouds painted on the ceiling. $

 B4 1518 E. 53RD ST.
773-667-0647

WALNUT ROOM

If power shopping at Marshall Field's flagship State Street store works up your appetite, take a lunch break for some comfort food in the regal seventh-floor Walnut Room. During the holiday season, the dark-paneled, old-world eatery showcases a towering Christmas tree. $$

 A2 111 N. STATE ST., 7TH FLOOR
312-781-3125

WAVE

This Aspen-chic restaurant hosts the partying Prada set and well-heeled business people alike. The superb Mediterranean-influenced menu proves that Wave has style and substance. The seafood sampler is a delight. $$

 C4 644 N. LAKE SHORE DR.
312-255-4460

WIENER CIRCLE

The louder and ruder you are, the better your chances of getting some food at this magnet for tipsy twentysomethings. Sinful cheese fries, all-beef franks, and plenty of one-liners are all served up at this late-night hot dog hut. $

 E4 2622 N. CLARK ST.
773-477-7444

WOLF & KETTLE COFFEE SHOP

Loyola University students mingle and loiter in this college coffeehouse, where the barren interior of weathered wooden tables and chairs is offset by resplendent stained glass windows. It's a refreshing alternative for Mag Mile shoppers trying to avoid the abundant chain cafés. $

 B2 101 E. PEARSON ST.
312-915-8595

ZOOM KITCHEN

This ultramodern chain, the height of cafeteria-chic, is accented with stainless steel and black-and-white Marc Hauser photographs. Custom-made salads and freshly carved meats feed a younger, fast food eschewing crowd. $

 C2 247 S. STATE ST.
312-377-9666

 C4 620 W. BELMONT AVE.
773-325-1400

Ⓢ SHOPS

DIRECTORY OF SHOPS

ACCENT CHICAGO

Expect to find a ubiquitous selection of Chicago souvenirs, including mugs, magnets, key chains, and T-shirts, along with a smattering of unique items, such as models of landmark buildings.

 C4 233 S. WACKER DR.
312-993-0499

AFROCENTRIC BOOKSTORE

African American literature is the focus, and the scope is wide: fiction, business, spiritual, and children's books. Prestigious authors have appeared for book signings here, including Colin Powell.

 C2 333 S. STATE ST.
312-939-1956

ALEX SEPKUS

This exclusive boutique carries Sepkus-designed brooches and bracelets, and especially his signature rings, ornately textured silver and gold pieces embedded with precious and semiprecious gems.

 A2 106 E. OAK ST.
312-440-0044

ALPHABÉTIQUE

This posh stationer is the exclusive Chicago distributor for Soolip Paperie & Press. Vellums, silk paper, and Egyptian papyrus come in a rainbow of hues.

 B2 701 W. ARMITAGE AVE.
312-751-2920

ALTERNATIVES

Stocking European styles at least a year before they hit department store racks, Alternatives carries Italian leather pumps, stiletto heels, and debonair men's shoes.

 A1 942 N. RUSH ST.
312-266-1545

AMERICAN GIRL PLACE

 With dolls in tote, Chicago girls congregate at this combination shop/café/theater, enjoying its wide selection of books, toys, Bitty Babies, big-kid gear, and matching outfits for girl and doll.

B2 111 E. CHICAGO AVE.
877-247-5223

ANCIENT ECHOES

Find unique jewelry with a spiritual bent among the home furnishings at Ancient Echoes. Friendly associates preside over Ayala Bar's beaded cross pendants, Mary Frances' ornate clutch purses, and Brandon Williams' whimsical furniture.

 B6 1003 W. ARMITAGE AVE.
773-880-1003

ANTHROPOLOGIE

Browse through racks of embellished jeans, frilly blouses, and lingerie from designers like Free People and Co-operative. Jewelry, bath products, knickknacks, and housewares occupy equal floor space in this rustic setting.

 F5 1120 N. STATE ST.
312-255-1848

ART EFFECT

Within the exposed brick walls of this sprawling store, you'll find Tote le Monde striped bags, Bloom lotions, retro kitchenware, and an eclectic assortment of clothes, including Three Dots tees and paisley '70s skirts.

 B6 934 W. ARMITAGE AVE.
773-929-3600

ARTISANS 21

A cooperative gallery run by local artists and located in the Harper Court shopping complex, Artisans 21 showcases works in stained glass, pottery, watercolor, and bronze – all for sale.

 B4 5225 S. HARPER AVE.
773-288-7450

BARBARA'S BOOKSTORE

 Open since 1963, this local independent chain remains a neighborhood favorite by hosting high-profile readings. The well-organized selection caters to a wide audience, with ample kids' and travel sections.

 E4 1350 N. WELLS ST.
312-642-5044

BARNES & NOBLE

This chain bookstore sets itself apart with a relaxed atmosphere that encourages browsing and a vast, well-organized selection.

Readings, book clubs, and signings take place on plush chairs with java from the in-store café.

 B4 1441 W. WEBSTER AVE.
773-871-3610

BLOMMER'S CHOCOLATE STORE

As part of the candy capital of the world, Blommer's duly contributes its own chocolaty aroma to the neighborhood. Look for the huge 10-pound bar – along with more moderately sized treats – in the gift shop.

 D3 600 W. KINZIE ST.
312-492-1336

BLUE CHICAGO STORE

Blues merchandise on offer includes shirts, posters, CDs, mugs, and prints by artist John Carroll Doyle. Check for the smoke-free, all-ages blues show held in the basement on Saturdays.

 D6 536 N. CLARK ST.
312-661-1003

BORDERS

This multilevel megastore manages to create a neighborhood vibe with its frequent readings, book signings, and a browser-friendly periodicals area. Also notable are the music, travel, cooking, and technology sections.

 E4 2817 N. CLARK ST.
773-935-3909

CAMBIUM

The handcrafted furniture and quality kitchenware at this store in the burgeoning River North home furnishings district will fit any décor. The knowledgeable staff provides personal attention.

D5 113-119 W. HUBBARD ST.
312-832-9920

CARSON PIRIE SCOTT & CO.

The 1898 flagship Carson Pirie Scott building was designed by Louis Sullivan and features an ornate cast-iron façade. The mammoth department store boasts exclusive clothing lines and a vast selection of housewares.

 B2 1 S. STATE ST.
312-641-7000

CHIAROSCURO

Hand-painted dog bowls, novelty barware, decorative stemware, whimsical lamps and mirrors, and other eye candy compete for your attention at this Chicago Place establishment.

 C2 700 N. MICHIGAN AVE.
312-988-9253

▲

CHIASSO

Emphasizing form and function, Chiasso stocks well-designed goods for every room in the house: Michael Graves teakettles, Octopus toothbrush holders, and ultramodern Philippe Starck serving trays.

 B2 835 N. MICHIGAN AVE.
312-280-1249

CITY SOLES

 A chic space decked out with paintings by local artists and mod furniture, City Soles and its adjoining, upscale sister store Niche, carry labels like Costume National and Gianfranco Ferre, respectively.

 D2 2001 W. NORTH AVE.
773-489-2001

CRATE & BARREL

Originating in Old Town, *the* home superstore occupies a flagship glass-and-concrete structure filled with simple, modern interpretations of every conceivable houseware item, plus a seasonal collection.

 D1 850 W. NORTH AVE.
312-573-9800

CROW'S NEST RECORDS

 A cut above its national competitors, this local chain offers a sterile but well-organized environment in which to browse through imports, rare finds, and new releases in every category.

 C2 333 S. STATE ST.
312-341-9196

CYNTHIA ROWLEY

Local designer Cynthia Rowley's girlie yet sophisticated fashions are a staple of celebrity wardrobes. Find the same wares – ranging from leather to frilly, purses to shoes – in her whimsical boutique.

 B1 808 W. ARMITAGE AVE.
773-528-6160

DAISY SHOP

Gently worn couture handbags, jewelry, and clothing draw a discerning clientele to this discreet Oak Street boutique. The sixth-floor shop features reduced prices on Chanel, Gucci, Louis Vuitton, and other fashion heavyweights.

 A1 67 E. OAK ST.
312-943-8880

DAVIS FOR MEN

Supplying stylish men with the latest suits and casual wear, Davis for Men stocks Dolce & Gabbana, Armani, and other European designers as well as an ample big-and-tall selection.

 D1 824 W. NORTH AVE.
312-266-9599

DR. WAX RECORDS

 This cluttered, poster-lined store holds rows of new vinyl and CDs, plus an assortment of used music in every genre, with an emphasis on hip-hop and all incarnations of jazz.

 B4 5225 S. HARPER AVE.
773-493-8696

ENDO-EXO APOTHECARY

Scrumptious bath products and cosmetics from New York's Bliss Spa, Sundari, and Delux line the glass shelves in this vibrant, aromatic shop. Wash off between applications at the courtesy sinks.

 B1 2034 N. HALSTED ST.
773-525-0500

EQUINOX

Tiffany and Paul Sahlin Mission lamps beckon passersby into this fantasy world of baubles, ornaments, candles, and furniture. Browse the overwhelming selection of seasonal items during the winter holidays.

 C4 3401 N. BROADWAY ST.
773-281-9151

ETRE

Freestanding wrought-iron racks hold Rebecca Taylor blazers and Vitamina jeans in a relaxed atmosphere pulsing with music. The superb shoe collection ranges from Jimmy Choo to Espace.

 E4 1361 N. WELLS ST.
312-266-8101

FABRICE

Peruse Parisian accessories – from Fabrice jewelry to Roger & Gallet soaps – in this bright, feminine boutique. Check out the bags in vividly hued paper or textured denim with interchangeable handles.

 D4 1714 N. WELLS ST.
312-280-0011

FANNIE MAY CANDIES

Since 1920, Fannie May has hooked patrons on its dark and milk chocolates, caramels, creams, dried fruits, and the signature Trinidad, a crunchy coconut-covered chocolate. Pick-and-mix boxes come beautifully wrapped.

 B2 130 S. WABASH AVE.
312-443-1018

FAO SCHWARZ

Kids of all ages will be entranced by the Gravity Loop, huge stuffed animals, self-propelling high-tech toys, and classic collectibles. Visit the live toy soldier at Christmastime.

 B2 840 N. MICHIGAN AVE.
312-587-5000

FISHMAN'S FABRICS

This 10,000-square-foot warehouse displays bolts of fabric for every conceivable creation. High-quality silk, faux fur, suede and leather, chenille, and chiffon take every color of the rainbow.

 E3 1101 S. DESPLAINES ST.
312-922-7250

FLASHY TRASH

 The perfect stop before a masquerade ball or a disco party, Flashy Trash purveys period costumes spanning the entire 20th century and contemporary duds by Diesel and Lip Service.

 B3 3524 N. HALSTED ST. 773-327-6900

FOURTH WORLD ARTISANS
The pounding rhythm of world beat permeates this shop filled with instruments, masks, textiles, sculptures, and rugs from across the globe, with countries like Haiti, Mexico, India, Guatemala, and Africa represented.

 C1 3440 N. SOUTHPORT AVE. 773-404-5200

FOX & OBEL
Akin to a New York food market, this upscale emporium carries prepared goods, including sushi and salads, as well as imported cheeses, herbs, oils, pastas, chocolates, and a selection of wine.

 D3 401 E. ILLINOIS ST. 312-410-7301

FOX'S
Bargain hunters flock to Fox's for its name-brand merchandise at discount prices – even if the designer tags have been removed – and for its constantly rotating selection of up-to-the-minute styles.

 B1 2150 N. HALSTED ST. 773-281-0700

GARRETT POPCORN SHOPS
Fans queue up for ages to get a bag of steaming popcorn liberally topped with cheddar, caramel, butter, or salt. No atmosphere or seating to speak of, just the aroma of popcorn.

 C1 2 W. JACKSON BLVD. 312-360-1108

 C2 670 N. MICHIGAN AVE. 312-944-2630

GIFTLAND
Find a vast collection of trinkets, from shot glasses to one-of-a-kind greeting cards to potted bamboo, in this cluttered shop. Head to the back for embroidered purses and Chinese silk dresses.

 D1 2212 S. WENTWORTH AVE. 312-225-0088

GISELA
Local jewelry designer Gisela showcases her unusual collection – rubber rings with inlaid diamonds, crocheted rings, tension rings and

bracelets – in a sculptural setting of glass, aluminum, and mirrors.

 A2 64 E. WALTON PLACE 312-944-5263

GOLDEN TRIANGLE
Southeast Asian antiques with an emphasis on functional pieces – armoires that can house a stereo, for example – include gems like 3,000-year-old terra cotta jars and Chinese apothecary cases, all arranged in room vignettes.

 D6 72 W. HUBBARD ST. 312-755-1266

HAMMACHER SCHLEMMER
 Pages from the famous catalog come to life in this store – one of two Hammacher Schlemmer retail shops in the country – where inventions for everyday use share space with futuristic gadgets.

 D2 445 N. MICHIGAN AVE. 312-527-9100

HANDLE WITH CARE
A wide array of clothing nestles within these mint-green walls. Sort through racks of Diane von Furstenberg, Trina Turk, and Weston Wear. Accessories cover all bases, from head to toe.

 D4 1706 N. WELLS ST. 312-751-2929

HOUSE OF GLUNZ
Open since 1888, this Victorian wine shop carries hundreds of vintages, from inexpensive everyday to rare finds dating from the early 1800s. Monthly tastings feature bottles from the private cellar.

 F4 1206 N. WELLS ST. 312-642-3000

HOYPOLOI GALLERY
Nestled among tchotchke shops and bakeries, Hoypoloi resembles an upscale gallery. Skagen watches, Dali-esque clocks, and hand-dyed silk scarves share the small space with Buddha sculptures and Chinese tea sets.

 D1 2235 S. WENTWORTH AVE. 312-225-6477

HUBBA-HUBBA

 This elegant space features casual, dressy, and some vintage pieces – think soft sweaters and 1940s-inspired dresses – as well as unusual purses and jewelry.

 C3 3309 N. CLARK ST. 773-477-1414

ISABELLA FINE LINGERIE

Owner Lauren Amerine chooses her high-quality merchandise carefully. Cosabella thongs, Eberjey pajamas, Paul Smith slips, nursing bras, and swimwear share drawer space in this inviting, olive-green store.

 B6 1101 W. WEBSTER AVE. 773-281-2352

JAZZ RECORD MART

The owner of the Delmark Records label runs this mart, which houses jazz and blues recordings of interest to both collectors and novices. Also find spoken word, gospel, and a variety of magazines.

 D1 444 N. WABASH AVE. 312-222-1467

JOLIE JOLI

Arranged according to the principles of Feng Shui, this inviting boutique carries tailored essentials for men and women: Isabel Marant for her, Ted Baker London for him, and New York Industrie for both.

 B4 2131 N. SOUTHPORT AVE. 773-327-4917

KATE SPADE

Her handbags are the passport to the tony Lincoln Park circuit, although the clean lines and simple aesthetics appeal to a wide audience. Shoes, paper, and fragrances augment the collection.

 A2 101 E. OAK ST. 312-654-8853

KIVA

Named after the sacred dwellings of the Anasazis, KIVA day spa emphasizes healing and rejuvenation in a soothing earth-toned atmosphere. Pampering regimens include aroma exfoliation massage, reflexology, and anti-cellulite treatment.

B2 196 E. PEARSON ST. 312-840-8120

THE LEGO STORE AND CONSTRUCTION ZONE

The classic toy gets royal treatment here with hard-to-find European products, a baby line, and a huge play zone with replicas of the Chicago skyline and a giant dinosaur.

 D2 520 N. MICHIGAN AVE. 312-494-0760

LILLE

Clean, white wall shelves and sleek, sturdy tables display an assortment of Dinosaur Designs resin accessories, Christian Tortu vases, local designer Amanda Larsen Puck jewelry, silk pillows, and retro clocks.

 D2 1923 W. NORTH AVE. 773-342-0563

LINCOLN ANTIQUE MALL

More than 10,000 square feet of treasures and castoffs run the gamut from expensive Victorian furniture to retro lunchboxes. Wander through this semi-organized oasis of clothing, decorative pieces, barware, and paintings.

 D1 3141 N. LINCOLN AVE. 773-244-1440

LMNOP

This spacious, kid-friendly store features a built-in dollhouse and cute outfits for infants to size 8. Find everything from playful prints to dress-up clothes by Cakewalk, Blue Dot, Lucky Fish, and Milk & Honey.

 F3 2574 N. LINCOLN AVE. 773-975-4055

LORI'S DESIGNER SHOES

Designer kicks line the walls, reach the ceiling, and draw crowds. Look for discounted Steve Madden, Via Spiga, Charles David, and more, from winter boots to strappy eveningwear, plus purses galore.

 B1 824 W. ARMITAGE AVE. 773-281-5655

LUMINAIRE

Contemporary European furnishings, such as linear couches by Jasper Morrison, H2O workstations, and Zettel'z paper suspension lamps, take center stage at this showroom for the modern home.

 C5 301 W. SUPERIOR ST. 312-664-9582

MADISON & FRIENDS

Trend-conscious kids – and their parents – will find Suss Design and Petit Bateau for girls, sports gear and tiny bomber jackets for boys, plus Shoe Be Doo shoes and Zooper strollers.

 A1 940 N. RUSH ST. 312-642-6403

MARSHALL FIELD'S

This landmark department store boasts the Great Clock, a Tiffany mosaic dome, eight floors filled with fashionable clothing and home goods, and the stately Walnut Room restaurant. Holiday window displays are memorable.

 A2 111 N. STATE ST. 312-781-1000

MATERIAL CULTURE

Displaying relics from the owners' world travels, these cramped quarters house antique Asian cabinets, ceramics, vases, and a few modern rugs. Take the elevator downstairs for the recent acquisitions.

 D5 401 N. LASALLE ST. 312-467-1490

MATERIAL POSSESSIONS

Artist-made home furnishings run the gamut from Jay Strongwater bejeweled picture frames and wooden jewelry boxes to Alchemy Metalworks pillar candleholders and glazed ceramic sushi place settings.

 B1 54 E. CHESTNUT ST. 312-280-4885

MODERNICA

Modernize your home with fiberglass shell chairs, Case Study modular shelving, and wire kitchen chairs. Books and videos pay homage to Eames, Herman Miller, and the like.

 D5 555 W. FRANKLIN ST. 312-222-1808

NO PLACE LIKE

White, exposed brick walls provide the backdrop for unique furniture, while suspended shelves display plates, vases, and a full range of dinnerware and stemware by European designers.

 D5 300 W. GRAND AVE. 312-822-0550

PAGODA RED

Tucked away behind a carved wooden door and an open-air entryway, this bilevel store feels like an emperor's lair, perfectly outfitted with antique Chinese red-lacquered cabinets, bamboo-and-fabric kites, Tibetan vases, and Buddha statues.

 D2 1714 N. DAMEN AVE. 773-235-1188

PAPER SOURCE

Three small floors burst with handmade paper in every imaginable color and texture, plus journals, cards, rubber stamps, and bookbinding materials. Printmaking classes are also offered here.

 B5 232 W. CHICAGO AVE. 312-337-0798

PAUL STUART

The well-tailored threads from Paul Stuart evoke images of London's Saville Row. Double-breasted pin stripe suits for him match tweed and cashmere separates for her. Or order made-to-measure dress shirts.

 B2 875 N. MICHIGAN AVE. 312-640-2650

P.45

 Lined with touchable apparel and versatile jewelry from up-and-coming designers – Susana Monaco, ARC-101, Me & Ro, Delilah, and Development – p.45's loftlike atmosphere welcomes leisurely browsing.

 D2 1643 N. DAMEN AVE. 773-862-4523

PIGGY TOES

The playful window display of tiny children's shoes sets the mood for stylish European creations, from infant booties to European size 38. Moccasins, gym shoes, and dressy styles suit small feet.

 B1 2205 N. HALSTED ST. 773-281-5583

PISTACHIOS

Jewelry, eyewear, salt-and-pepper shakers, and other contemporary crafts share display space in this quiet, gallerylike setting.

 D1 55 E. GRAND AVE.
312-595-9437

POWELL'S BOOK STORE

Academic and scholarly works take precedence at Powell's three Chicago locations. The Hyde Park store features a quarter of a million used, discounted, and rare titles, including Oxford University Press reprints.

 D4 1501 E. 57TH ST.
773-955-7780

▲

PRAIRIE AVENUE BOOKSHOP

Architecture buffs may get lost among the stacks of books on buildings, design, urban studies, landscaping, and technical codes. The shop's interior was inspired by the Chicago and Prairie schools.

 C2 418 S. WABASH AVE.
312-922-8311

PRINTER'S ROW FINE & RARE BOOKS

This antiquarian bookstore, designed by architect Wilbert R. Hasbrouck, sits on historic Printer's Row. Its selection of rare editions of 19th- and 20th-century fiction caters to collectors.

 D6 715 S. DEARBORN ST.
312-583-1800

QUIMBY'S

A hip clientele congregates at

 Quimby's for its hard-to-find 'zines, salacious titles, comics, and distinct selection of fiction, non-fiction, and poetry, including numerous titles on body artistry. Readings are held frequently.

 D3 1854 W. NORTH AVE.
773-342-0910

RAND MCNALLY MAP & TRAVEL

A draw for travelers of every stripe, this multipurpose travel store sells guidebooks, maps for nearly every city and country, compact travel packs, language converters, and global positioning systems.

 B4 150 S. WACKER DR.
312-332-2009

RECKLESS RECORDS

Local indie titles abound, as do albums produced by Chicago legend Steve Albini. Try out a jazz, punk, or ambient CD at a listening station before investing. Or choose from the nostalgic vinyl selection.

 D2 1532 N. MILWAUKEE AVE.
773-235-3727

SALON 1800 AND HAVEN SPA

Salon 1800 provides full-service hair care, makeup application, and spa manicures and pedicures. Haven Spa, located across the street, offers Swedish, stone, and "aqua-bliss" massages.

 B6 1011 W. ARMITAGE AVE.
773-929-6010

SAM'S WINE & SPIRITS

Sam's knowledgeable staff will help you find the perfect vintage in this huge liquor emporium, which stocks wines by grape and region as well as champagne, beer, accessories, cheeses, and gift baskets.

 C6 1720 N. MARCEY ST.
312-664-4394

THE SAVVY TRAVELLER

 With a focus on guides and literature for niche and exotic travelers, Savvy caters to backpackers, gay vacationers, business travelers, and everyone in between. Find travel gear, too.

 C2 310 S. MICHIGAN AVE.
312-913-9800

SEMINARY CO-OP BOOKSTORE

With branches at 57th Street Books and in the Newberry Library, the original Co-op is famous among bibliophiles for its rarefied selection of novels, nonfiction, and academic journals. Members save 10 percent.

 D2 5757 S. UNIVERSITY AVE.
773-752-4381

SHOE SOUL

Sergio Rossi, Krizia, and other fashionable Italian kicks line the shelves at Shoe Soul. Don't expect to find multiple sizes of each style, but do expect high quality, fine leather, and uncommon designs.

 C4 3243 N. BROADWAY ST. 773-388-1100

SILVER MOON

Stucco walls, worn floorboards, and Roaring '20s music set the tone for vintage wedding dresses, designer clothing, feather boas, and rhinestone jewelry. A separate room features eclectic home accessories.

 C3 3337 N. HALSTED ST. 773-883-0222

SOFIE

Choose among the selection of unique clothes including trousers, peasant blouses, and screen-printed tees, then duck behind one of the three cream-colored curtains/dressing chambers to try on the threads.

 E4 1343 N. WELLS ST. 312-255-1343

SPA SPACE

Cool down after a deep-tissue massage or grape-seed body scrub with a "rainshower" in Spa Space's serene environment. Advanced procedures include microdermabrasion and sea enzyme body-firming treatment.

 F4 161 N. CANAL ST. 312-466-9585

THE SPICE HOUSE

Freshly ground imported and domestic spices create a pervasive aroma. Ceylon cinnamon, sea salts, Tahitian vanilla, Mexican epazote, black sesame seeds, and spice blends come in plain, sturdy packaging.

 E4 1512 N. WELLS ST. 312-274-0378

STRANGE CARGO

Slightly musty and chock-full of odd and arcane treasures, Strange Cargo stocks '50s through '80s nostalgia – attention-getting T-shirts, wigs, used jeans, bowling shirts – and some new clothing.

 C3 3448 N. CLARK ST. 773-327-8090

TENDER BUTTONS

Buttons, including cameos, silver, Bakelite, mother-of-pearl, animal-shaped, and run-of-the-mill plastic, polka-dot the walls of this unique museum/shop. Visitors often find themselves lost in the minutiae.

 A1 946 N. RUSH ST. 312-337-7033

TEN REN TEA & GINSENG CO.

Medicinal herbs and jars of loose tea, from gunpowder to rare oolongs, line the shelves in this welcoming store and teahouse. Sample a trendy bubble tea with chewy tapioca pearls.

 D1 2247 S. WENTWORTH AVE. 312-842-1171

TERRAIN

This earth-toned store stocks botanical-based products with a conscience: environmentally friendly and no animal testing. Get Fresh, Terax, Kiehl's, and Terrain's own product line fill the apothecary's shelves.

 F3 2542 N. HALSTED ST. 773-549-0888

TIFFANI KIM INSTITUTE

Tiffani Kim extends its salon, spa, and wellness institute to offer complete, one-stop service for brides, from gown and veil fittings to day-of makeup application. Private treatment rooms available.

C5 310 W. SUPERIOR ST. 312-943-8777

TIME WELL

You can't miss this corner warehouse/consignment store, with its wide glass windows displaying Depression-era and newer furniture. Side tables, dining sets, sofas, and other pieces stand the test of time.

 E2 2780 N. LINCOLN AVE. 773-549-2113

TRAGICALLY HIP

On a bustling, crowded street, find this fashionable haven for the well-dressed pre-teen to professional. Girly prints and tailored frocks share the bubble gum–pink space.

 C3 931 W. BELMONT AVE.
773-549-1500

TROTTER'S TO GO

Celebrity chef Charlie Trotter opened this store for time-pressed foodies. Find premium organic and seasonal products, spit-roasted game, salads, artisan cheeses, hand-made chocolates, olives, and an extensive wine selection.

 A5 1337 W. FULLERTON AVE.
773-868-6510

TRUEFITT & HILL

In the *Guinness Book of World Records* as the world's oldest bar-bershop, circa 1805, this Chicago branch of the "gentlemen's per-fumer and hairdresser" offers such services as hot lather shaves and men's manicures.

 A2 900 N. MICHIGAN AVE.
312-337-2525

ULTIMO

This store put Dolce & Gabbana and Armani on the Chicago map. The trademark antler light fixtures remain, but fashion-forward designers – think Robert Danes – are the focus now.

 A2 114 E. OAK ST.
312-787-1171

UNABRIDGED BOOKS

An inviting, two-level store, Unabridged carries a complete selection of gay and lesbian titles as well as children's books, the latest fiction, and travel guides. Look for the personal reviews tacked on shelves.

 C4 3251 N. BROADWAY ST.
773-883-9119

UNCLE FUN

New merchandise crops up frequent-ly from Uncle Fun's globetrotting journeys, so shelves overflow with plastic figurines, inflatable toys, oversized sunglasses, jack-in-the-boxes, tiaras, and gags.

 C2 1338 W. BELMONT AVE.
773-477-8223

URBAN OASIS

Complimentary herbal teas and fruit juices, private changing rooms, and kimonos set the stage for first-class spa treatments, including salt glow and reflexology, in a space that embodies the Japanese aesthetic.

 A6 12 W. MAPLE ST.
312-587-3500

VIRTU

Scented candles permeate this tiny boutique, which carries delicate, ethereal goods. Colorful glassware, sculptural jewelry, petite metalwork handbags, and organic-looking ceramics sit beside handmade wrap-ping paper and cards.

 B2 2034 N. DAMEN AVE.
773-235-3790

VOSGES HAUT-CHOCOLAT

Exotic ingredients and fragrant spices, such as curry powder, Japanese wasabi, and kaffir lime, add an unusual depth of flavor to these sinful chocolate truffles. Exclusive chocolatier for Le Cordon Bleu.

 D2 520 N. MICHIGAN AVE.
312-644-9450

WABASH JEWELERS MALL

Dozens of jeweler stalls glitter with diamonds, gold, and silver, and most of the artisans will create unique pieces on spec. Relax at the Middle Eastern lunch spot, Oasis Cafe, between browsings.

 B2 21 N. WABASH AVE.
312-263-1757

WAXMAN CANDLES

Drippy, layered, floating, spiral, tapered, votive, and scented candles are made on the premises and housed in a fragrant room dominat-ed by clever candle holders and wax creations.

 D1 3044 N. LINCOLN AVE.
773-929-3000

Ⓐ **AMUSEMENTS**

MUSEUMS AND GALLERIES

▲

ADLER PLANETARIUM AND ASTRONOMY MUSEUM
See SIGHTS, p. 2.

 F6 1300 S. LAKE SHORE DR.
312-922-7827

AMERICAN BAR ASSOCIATION MUSEUM
This museum at the ABA headquarters features exhibits on the important, and sometimes sensational, trials of the past two centuries, from *Brown v. Board of Education* to Watergate to O.J. Simpson.

 B4 750 N. LAKE SHORE DR.
312-988-6222

ARON PACKER GALLERY
The Aron Packer champions outsider art (made by self-taught artists), a major part of the Chicago art scene, as well as folk and contemporary works in all media.

A2 118 N. PEORIA ST.
312-226-8984

AROUND THE COYOTE/ATC SPACE
As well as sponsoring the popular annual tour of studios in arty Wicker Park, ATC features rising local contemporary artists in its space in the historic Flat Iron Arts Building.

 D2 1579 N. MILWAUKEE AVE.
773-342-6777

ART INSTITUTE OF CHICAGO
See SIGHTS, p. 4.

B2 111 S. MICHIGAN AVE.
312-443-3600

ARTS CLUB OF CHICAGO
This storied contemporary art gallery, which features a Mies van der Rohe-designed stairwell, offers five free exhibits a year. In the 1920s, the Arts Club was Picasso's first venue in Chicago.

 C2 201 E. ONTARIO ST.
312-787-3997

BETTY RYMER GALLERY AT THE SCHOOL OF THE ART INSTITUTE

 The primary on-site gallery at this renowned school features cutting-edge works in the visual arts by students and faculty, as well as other local and national artists.

 B3 280 S. COLUMBUS DR.
312-443-3703

CARL HAMMER
Since opening in 1979, this gallery built its name by focusing on contemporary American and European outsider artists, like actor/comedian Martin Mull, and helped bring the genre into the mainstream.

 C5 740 N. WELLS ST.
312-266-8512

CATHERINE EDELMAN GALLERY
An established outlet for contemporary photography, the Edelman changes its exhibits of local and national talent about every six weeks. Missed one? Prints from many past shows can be viewed upon request.

 C5 300 W. SUPERIOR ST., LOWER LEVEL 312-266-2350

CHICAGO ARCHITECTURE CENTER
Located in the Burnham-designed Santa Fe building, the Chicago Architecture Center maintains a grand-scale model of the Chicago skyline, along with a timeline of the city's important architectural developments.

 C2 224 S. MICHIGAN AVE.
312-922-3432

CHICAGO ATHENAEUM
This museum espousing "good design" keeps a permanent collection of industrial and graphic design arts and architectural plans. Its exhibit themes can range from kites to modern quilts.

 E2 307 N. MICHIGAN AVE.
312-372-1083

CHICAGO CENTER FOR BOOK & PAPER ARTS

This Columbia College-based program has a gallery displaying the best in books, fine binding, paper sculpture, papermaking, printing, decorative paper, calligraphy, and lettering.

 E2 1104 S. WABASH AVE., 2ND FL. 312-344-6630

CHICAGO CULTURAL CENTER

See SIGHTS, p. 7.

 A2 78 E. WASHINGTON ST. 312-346-3278

CHICAGO HISTORICAL SOCIETY

 The state's multicultural past comes alive here through inventive exhibitions and collections that include artifacts from the Great Fire and the belongings of Illinoisan Abraham Lincoln. Among them, an original copy of the 13th Amendment.

 D4 1601 N. CLARK ST. 312-642-4600

CITY GALLERY

Located inside the historic Water Tower, this gallery displays free, changing exhibits of Chicago-themed photography by local artists.

 B2 806 N. MICHIGAN AVE. 312-742-0808

CLARKE HOUSE MUSEUM

 Billed as Chicago's oldest home, the Clarke House-turned-museum is one of the city's few pre-Civil War buildings still standing, though not in its original location – it's been moved twice in its lifetime.

 C3 1827 S. INDIANA AVE. 312-745-0040

DAVID AND ALFRED SMART MUSEUM OF ART

Like the Art Institute, this museum covers a broad range – from ancient Greek vases to Frank Lloyd Wright's Robie House dining table to Degas sculptures – but the well-edited displays allow for quick visits.

 C2 5550 S. GREENWOOD AVE. 773-702-0200

DOUGLAS DAWSON

Known nationally for its collection of ethnographic art from Africa, Southeast Asia, South Pacific, and China, Douglas Dawson showcases rare finds like a 16th-century Burmese stone footprint of Buddha and African tribal textiles.

 C5 222 W. HURON ST. 312-751-1961

DUSABLE MUSEUM OF AFRICAN AMERICAN HISTORY

The first U.S. museum dedicated to the African American experience, the DuSable tells the story with historic artifacts, from original slave documents to civil rights memorabilia. It displays African art and 19th- and 20th-century paintings, also.

 D1 740 E. 56TH PLACE 773-947-0600

FIELD MUSEUM OF NATURAL HISTORY

See SIGHTS, p. 11.

 F4 1400 S. LAKE SHORE DR. 312-922-9410

FRANK LLOYD WRIGHT HOME AND STUDIO

 See the inception of the Prairie style at the first home of this distinctly American architect. In addition, 25 buildings designed by Wright grace the village around the museum. Nine miles west of downtown.

OFF MAP OAK PARK 951 CHICAGO AVE. 708-848-1976

GLESSNER HOUSE MUSEUM

 Representative of Chicago's Gilded Age, this historic home is a trove of decorative arts with its oak-paneled interior, William Morris textiles, and other items from the Glessner family's original furnishings.

 C3 1800 S. PRAIRIE AVE. 312-326-1480

INTERNATIONAL MUSEUM OF SURGICAL SCIENCE

This museum of surgical history is not for the weak of stomach. Housed in a historic lakefront mansion, the collections include four-millennia-old Peruvian head surgery tools and an iron lung.

 D5 1524 N. LAKE SHORE DR. 312-642-6502

INTUIT

A nonprofit organization that focuses on untrained artists, Intuit is in the center of Chicago's thriving outsider art scene. The gallery offers classes, exhibits, and listings of other events nationwide.

 C1 756 N. MILWAUKEE AVE. 312-243-9088

JANE ADDAMS HULL HOUSE MUSEUM

The prominent early 20th-century social reformer Jane Addams formed her first community settlement at the Hull Mansion, which has been restored as a museum run by the University of Illinois at Chicago.

 D2 800 S. HALSTED AVE. 312-413-5353

JEAN ALBANO ART GALLERY

Showcasing paintings and conceptual pieces, Albano focuses on American artists, and her roster includes many well-known Chicagoans.

 C5 215 W. SUPERIOR ST. 312-440-0770

JOHN G. SHEDD AQUARIUM

See SIGHTS, p. 15.

 F4 1200 S. LAKE SHORE DR. 312-939-2435

MEXICAN FINE ARTS CENTER MUSEUM

This museum representing Mexican and Mexican American contributions expanded its permanent collection space in 2002. You'll find everything from figurines from 350 B.C. Mexico to photographs of the Mexican Revolution.

OVERVIEW MAP D3 1852 W. 19TH ST. 312-738-1503

MUSEUM OF BROADCAST COMMUNICATIONS

The diversions here include access to more than 70,000 hours of archived classic TV and radio shows and commercials and the opportunity to play Harry Caray by calling a mock Cubs game.

 A2 CHICAGO CULTURAL CENTER, 78 E. WASHINGTON ST. 312-629-6000

MUSEUM OF CONTEMPORARY ART

See SIGHTS, p. 18.

 B3 220 E. CHICAGO AVE. 312-280-2660

MUSEUM OF CONTEMPORARY PHOTOGRAPHY

Focusing on post-1959 U.S. commercial and art photography, the MCP collection includes works by Paul Strand and Ansel Adams. Exhibits change about every two months.

 D2 600 S. MICHIGAN AVE. 312-663-5554

MUSEUM OF SCIENCE AND INDUSTRY

See SIGHTS, p. 19.

 D5 5700 S. LAKE SHORE DR. 773-684-1414 OR 800-468-6674

NATIONAL VIETNAM VETERANS ART MUSEUM

This museum showcases more than 700 works created by Vietnam veterans, who use various media to express their individual experiences. North Vietnamese and Viet Cong weaponry are on display as well.

 C3 1801 S. INDIANA AVE. 312-326-0270

NEWBERRY LIBRARY

This large humanities library's extensive collection of rare and historic books includes displayed maps and manuscripts, from a 1524 colored map of Mexico City to the Book of Kells.

 B6 60 W. WALTON ST. 312-943-9090

ORIENTAL INSTITUTE

This University of Chicago museum features art and artifacts (some garnered through university-sponsored archaeological digs) from ancient Egypt, Turkey, Iran, Iraq, Israel, and Syria.

 D3 1155 E. 58TH ST. 773-702-9514

PEGGY NOTEBAERT NATURE MUSEUM

Situated on Lincoln Park's North Pond, this hands-on museum celebrates the ecosystem with attractions like the open-all-year Butterfly Haven and its assortment of rare prairie plants and animals.

 F6 2430 N. CANNON DR.
773-755-5100

POLISH MUSEUM OF AMERICA

Located in the neighborhood that many Polish immigrants helped to settle, the museum centers around art and cultural items from Poland and the Polish American community.

 F5 984 MILWAUKEE AVE.
773-384-3352

RENAISSANCE SOCIETY

An outlet for the avant-garde scene since 1915, the spacious location on the University of Chicago campus continues to spotlight cutting-edge artists from the U.S. and Europe.

 D2 5811 S. ELLIS AVE.
773-702-8670

RHONA HOFFMAN

One of Chicago's most prestigious galleries, the Hoffman has shown big names like Cindy Sherman and Sol LeWitt. Its current location has solidified the West Loop Gate's reputation as an art destination.

 A2 118 N. PEORIA ST.
312-455-1990

ROBERT HENRY ADAMS FINE ART

The gallery features modern American paintings, drawings, and sculpture by early to mid-20th century artists, including giants such as Edward Hopper and Man Ray.

 C5 715 N. FRANKLIN ST.
312-642-8700

SMITH MUSEUM OF STAINED GLASS WINDOWS

The only U.S. museum exclusively devoted to stained glass, the Smith Museum features both religious and secular works, some from the likes of Frank Lloyd Wright and Louis Comfort Tiffany.

 D6 NAVY PIER, 600 E. GRAND AVE.
312-595-5024

SPERTUS MUSEUM

 Displaying 3,500 years of Jewish culture, religion, and art, the Spertus houses the first permanent U.S. Holocaust Memorial and a recreated Middle Eastern archaeological dig site.

 D2 618 S. MICHIGAN AVE.
312-322-1747

TERRA MUSEUM OF AMERICAN ART

 Works by American artists, including Whistler, Homer, O'Keeffe, and Hopper, are displayed in an open, easily navigable space. Particularly notable is the American Impressionism collection featuring Cassatt.

 C2 664 N. MICHIGAN AVE.
312-664-3939

WOMAN MADE

This nonprofit gallery features free exhibits of works mostly by women artists, both established and self-taught, in various media. Exhibit themes can range from surrealism to social topics like domestic violence.

 C3 1900 S. PRAIRIE AVE.
312-328-0038

WOOD STREET GALLERY & SCULPTURE GARDEN

A cornerstone of the Wicker Park gallery scene, Wood Street primarily showcases sculpture by both established and up-and-coming artists. The 8,500-square-foot garden is a delight in good weather.

 E3 1239 N. WOOD ST.
773-227-3306

ZOLLA-LIEBERMAN GALLERY

This pioneering gallery anchored this area's transition from a shaky neighborhood into the renowned River North Gallery District. It continues to show provocative contemporary painting, sculpture, and multimedia art.

C5 325 W. HURON ST.
312-944-1990

PERFORMING ARTS

ATHENAEUM THEATRE
Built in 1911, the Athenaeum now offers a wide range of programming, from plays and musicals to Chicago Improv Festival events.

 D1 2936 N. SOUTHPORT AVE.
773-935-6860

AUDITORIUM THEATRE
 Since Adler and Sullivan built this opulent, acoustically perfect theater in 1889, high-profile dance presentations, concerts, and big-ticket musicals have performed beneath its gilded, light-studded arches.

 C2 50 E. CONGRESS PKWY.
312-922-2110

BAILIWICK ARTS CENTER
Known for tackling issues from sexuality to race, Bailiwick stages experimental theater, including musicals and one-act plays. Ongoing series focus on gay, lesbian, and deaf topics.

 C2 1229 W. BELMONT AVE.
773-883-1090

BLUES HEAVEN FOUNDATION
Willie Dixon's Chess Records Studio is now a center for blues preservation and education. Hear local legends perform in the Blues Garden every summer.

 D3 2120 S. MICHIGAN AVE.
312-808-1286

BRIAR STREET THEATRE
Originally built as a carriage house and converted into a proscenium theater in the 1980s, Briar Street hosts a number of long-running shows, including the Blue Man Group.

 D3 3133 N. HALSTED ST.
773-348-4000

▲

CADILLAC PALACE THEATRE
The Versailles-inspired Palace originally opened in 1926 as a vaudeville theater and later became a movie house. Renovations in 1999 completed the transformation into the Cadillac, which now mounts big-ticket musicals.

 A5 151 W. RANDOLPH ST.
312-977-1700

CHICAGO CENTER FOR THE PERFORMING ARTS
This acting- and music-education facility stages productions at its multivenue center. Both students and Broadway stars have graced the intimate 350-seat main stage.

 C2 777 N. GREEN ST.
312-327-2000

CHICAGO SHAKESPEARE THEATER
Artistic director Barbara Gaines and visiting luminaries, such as Peter Brook, direct the Bard's best in this Elizabethan courtyard theater. An upstairs, black-box theater stages other works.

 D6 NAVY PIER, 800 E. GRAND AVE.
312-595-5600

CHICAGO SYMPHONY ORCHESTRA / SYMPHONY CENTER
 Under the baton of Daniel Barenboim, the Chicago Symphony Orchestra calls Symphony Center its home. The Center's world-renowned offerings range from classical to jazz to special events – and American-French food at the on-site Rhapsody restaurant.

 B2 220 S. MICHIGAN AVE.
312-294-3000

CHICAGO THEATER

See SIGHTS, p. 10.

 A6 175 N. STATE ST.
312-263-1138

CHOPIN THEATRE

Chopin's two stages host nationally acclaimed theater and Around the Coyote arts festival events. The Guild Complex, a literary arts organization, resides downstairs.

 F4 1543 W. DIVISION ST.
773-278-1500

COURT THEATRE

Since 1955, the University of Chicago's theater offshoot has staged works by Molière, Chekhov, Coward, and other classic playwrights, with two plays in rotating repertory annually.

 D2 5535 S. ELLIS AVE.
773-753-4472

DANCE CENTER OF COLUMBIA COLLEGE

Columbia College Chicago's dance program resides in a 33,000-square-foot art deco facility. Local and international contemporary dancers perform in the 272-seat theater and seven studios.

 A3 1306 S. MICHIGAN AVE.
312-344-8300

DOC FILMS AT THE UNIVERSITY OF CHICAGO

The long-running *Doc Films* series screens cinematic classics, foreign films, and documentaries every night of the academic year at the Max Palevsky Cinema in Ida Noyes Hall.

 E3 1212 E. 59TH ST.
773-702-8575

FACETS MULTIMEDIA

Combining a cinémathèque, an expansive video/DVD rental collection, and a film school, Facets showcases the best of non-multiplex fare – domestic and foreign flicks – and filmmaker appearances.

 A4 1517 W. FULLERTON AVE.
773-281-4114

FORD CENTER FOR THE PERFORMING ARTS/ ORIENTAL THEATRE

The Oriental Theatre opened in 1926 as a movie palace with a Far East décor. Now renamed the Ford Center

for the Performing Arts, it stages live musicals.

 A6 24 W. RANDOLPH ST.
312-977-1700

GENE SISKEL FILM CENTER

 Named after the late *Chicago Tribune* film critic with the famous thumb, the Art Institute's film center is home to premieres, retrospectives, revivals, and festival screenings.

 F1 164 N. STATE ST.
312-846-2600

GOODMAN THEATRE

 Under the direction of Robert Falls, the nationally acclaimed Goodman invites stage and screen to grace its Albert and Owen theaters. Performances include classic plays, new works, and one-person shows.

 A6 170 N. DEARBORN ST.
312-443-3800

HOTHOUSE (CENTER FOR INTERNATIONAL PERFORMANCE AND EXHIBITION)

HotHouse programming runs the gamut, from the freeform jazz of 8 Bold Souls to salsa lessons to film screenings. A two-drink minimum supports the vibrant nonprofit organization.

 D2 31 E. BALBO AVE.
312-362-9707

HOT TIX

Half-price, day-of-performance tickets are available for various productions at more than 125 venues. Tickets must be purchased in person. Closed Mondays.

 A6 78 W. RANDOLPH ST.

 B2 163 E. PEARSON ST.

IMPROVOLYMPIC

Witness a Harold – long-form, interweaving improvisational theater – in the Cabaret or a sketch comedy in the Del Close Theater. Famous alumni include Andy Dick and Tina Fey.

 B3 3541 N. CLARK ST.
773-880-0199

JOFFREY BALLET

 This internationally renowned ballet ensemble nails both cutting-edge and classical performances. When in Chicago, they can be seen in the Auditorium Theatre.

 C2 50 E. CONGRESS PKWY. 312-739-0120

LANDMARK'S CENTURY CENTRE CINEMA

Snuggle into comfy stadium seating with gourmet goodies while watching independent and foreign flicks that probably operated on lower budgets than Landmark does.

 E4 2828 N. CLARK ST. 773-248-7744

LOOKINGGLASS THEATRE COMPANY

In residence at the Ruth Page Center, this talented ensemble creates multimedia, physically demanding works, often about Chicago history. Moving to the historic Water Tower and Pumping Station in March 2003.

 A6 RUTH PAGE CENTER: 1016 N. DEARBORN ST. 773-477-8088

LYRIC OPERA OF CHICAGO

 The throne-shaped, art nouveau Civic Opera House is the permanent home of the Lyric, which counts Samuel Ramey and conductor Andrew Davis among its legendary company.

 B4 20 N. WACKER DR. 312-332-2244

MERCURY THEATER

Productions by smaller ensembles, musicals, and children's shows are typical fare at this 299-seat theater, which first opened as a nickelodeon in 1912.

 A1 3745 N. SOUTHPORT AVE. 773-325-1700

MUSIC BOX THEATRE

 This restored 1929 theater – a recreated palazzo complete with twinkling ceiling lights and organist – shows first-run foreign and independent films and sing-along classics.

 A1 3733 N. SOUTHPORT AVE. 773-871-6604

OLD TOWN SCHOOL OF FOLK MUSIC

The renowned Old Town hosts folk, world music, and kids' concerts, plus classes ranging from conga drumming to hula.

 OVERVIEW MAP A3 4544 N. LINCOLN AVE. 773-728-6000

THE OPRAH WINFREY SHOW

A former armory now houses multi-zillionaire Oprah Winfrey's Harpo Studios. Tapings generally take place Tuesdays, Wednesdays, and Thursdays. Reserve tickets a month in advance.

 A1 1058 W. WASHINGTON BLVD. 312-591-9222

PARK WEST

Comedians, rock bands, and World Music Festival performers converge on this theater and concert venue adjacent to Lincoln Park. Arrive early and snag a booth.

 B3 322 W. ARMITAGE AVE. 312-440-9191

PIPER'S ALLEY

See an independent film in the cinema; visit Donny's Skybox Studio for experimental theater and improv; or witness *Tony 'n' Tina's Wedding*, an interactive dinner theater.

 D4 1608 N. WELLS ST. 312-642-7500

REDMOON THEATER

This company's puppeteers and actors create vivid spectacles with masks, shadow puppets, and music, reinterpreting classic works and staging an annual All Hallows' Eve celebration. Call for schedule and location information.

 D1 2936 N. SOUTHPORT AVE. 773-388-9031

ROYAL GEORGE THEATRE

This four-theater complex does multiple duty as the home of long-running plays like *Late Nite Catechism*, host to high-profile premieres, and circuit stop for comedy tours.

D1 1641 N. HALSTED ST. 312-988-9000

RUTH PAGE CENTER FOR THE ARTS

This performing arts center and dance school, named after the dancer and choreographer who founded it, hosts innovative plays and dance performances by students and artists in residence.

 A6 1016 N. DEARBORN ST.
312-337-6543

SECOND CITY

 This "temple of satire" sparked the careers of Mike Nichols and John Belushi. See the scripted main stage or the lightning-fast improv.

 D4 1616 N. WELLS ST.
312-337-3992

SHUBERT THEATRE

 The tallest building in the city when it opened in 1906, the former Majestic Theatre hosts an array of classic plays and new musicals.

 B6 22 W. MONROE ST.
312-977-1700

STEPPENWOLF THEATRE COMPANY

The collaborative efforts of the ensemble, which includes Gary Sinise and John Malkovich, result in acclaimed new and classic plays. Off the main stage, the Garage and Studio theaters present challenging experimental works.

 D1 1650 N. HALSTED ST.
312-335-1650

STOREFRONT THEATER AT GALLERY 37 FOR THE ARTS

A nonprofit educational center, the Storefront houses a black-box space for performance art, puppetry, improv, hip-hop music theater, and staged readings.

 A2 66 E. RANDOLPH ST.
312-742-8497

THEATRE BUILDING CHICAGO

 A revolving door for numerous struggling theater ensembles and home to longer-running shows like

Hellcab, the Theatre Building features three stages, each with 148 seats.

 C2 1225 W. BELMONT AVE.
773-327-5252

THREE ARTS CLUB OF CHICAGO

Established in 1912 to support women in the three arts – literary, performance, and visual – this club currently hosts Landmark Jazz and Salon Series events.

 F5 1300 N. DEARBORN PKWY.
312-944-6250

▲

TOMMY GUN'S GARAGE

Gangsters and flappers re-create a Roaring '20s speakeasy while theater patrons feast on prime rib or lasagna and occasionally join the action on stage.

 F2 1239 S. STATE ST.
773-728-2828

VIC THEATRE

Stop in for a concert or attend *Brew & View,* a second-run and cult-film series. All three bars remain open during screenings.

 D3 3145 N. SHEFFIELD AVE.
312-618-8439

VICTORY GARDENS THEATER

The site of numerous world premieres, primarily by Chicago playwrights, this complex also hosts up-and-coming ensembles, such as Roadworks Productions and Remybumppo.

 A2 2257 N. LINCOLN AVE.
773-871-3000

WING & GROOVE THEATER COMPANY

In the historic Flat Iron Arts Building, Wing & Groove presents accessible original works by emerging artists and unusual reinterpretations of classic works.

 D2 1935½ W. NORTH AVE.
773-782-9416

NIGHTLIFE

ANDY'S JAZZ CLUB
On a lower street near shopping paradise Michigan Avenue, Andy's features jazz sets throughout the day. Its full menu attracts an after-work crowd.

 D1 11 E. HUBBARD ST.
312-642-6805

BERLIN
Anything goes and everyone is welcome at this dance club for gays, heteros, and transvestites. Bar murals pay homage to German cabarets.

 C3 954 W. BELMONT AVE.
773-348-4975

▲

BUDDY GUY'S LEGENDS
An array of memorabilia, including his polka-dot guitar, adorns blues icon Buddy Guy's club, which attracts top-notch musicians and an international crowd. Enjoy the extensive Cajun menu.

 D2 754 S. WABASH AVE.
312-427-0333

BUTCH MCGUIRE'S
A mainstay on the Division Street singles scene since the '60s reign of Hugh Hefner, Butch McGuire's packs in sports fans and rowdy pub crawlers.

 F5 20 W. DIVISION ST.
312-337-9080

CIRCUS
Nightclub impresario Billy Dec plays Barnum at this over-the-top big top. Acrobats perform gravity-defying acts above the dance floor, while patrons perch at tables along the circumference.

D6 901 W. WEED ST.
312-266-1200

CLUB ALPHONSE
Though it wouldn't survive in lounge-glutted River North, Club Alphonse maintains a steady stream of regulars with its drink specials, deejays, and a mellow – if sparse – atmosphere.

 A3 1351 S. MICHIGAN AVE.
312-697-0975

COQ D'OR
 Sip a top-shelf Executive martini in a smoke-steeped red leather booth at this classic, old-fashioned lounge located in the historic Drake Hotel.

 A2 140 E. WALTON PLACE
312-787-2200

COTTON CLUB
A tribute to the Harlem Renaissance era, this swank South Side club's Cab Calloway stage pleases jazz and blues aficionados, while a separate room pumps hip-hop rhythms.

 B3 1710 S. MICHIGAN AVE.
312-341-9787

CROBAR
Dennis Rodman may have left the building, but the wild crowd still throbs into the wee hours at this mega-club. Dress to impress to make the cut.

 D6 1543 N. KINGSBURY ST.
312-413-7000

DANNY'S TAVERN
Danny's unassuming exterior hides a relaxed lounge with a musical backdrop of cutting-edge tunes. The hip local crowd kicks back with strong, reasonably priced drinks.

 B2 1951 W. DICKENS AVE.
773-489-6457

DEJA VU
A black-and-white checkerboard floor, old rock posters, and mirrors comprise this bar's minimal décor. Patrons – mostly young professionals – arrive late and leave in pairs.

 E3 2624 N. LINCOLN AVE.
773-871-0205

DOUBLE DOOR

Double Door draws a variety of local and national acts, many of them hard rocking. Watch the stage action on video monitors while shooting pool downstairs.

 D2 1572 N. MILWAUKEE AVE.
773-489-3160

DRAGON ROOM

Hidden in a warehouse, this Asian-themed club has thumping bass-driven techno music and alcoves for concealing celebrities and locals alike. There's a back-room sushi and sake bar, too.

 E1 809 W. EVERGREEN ST.
312-751-2900

FADÓ

Gaelic for "long ago," Fadó's décor comes directly from Ireland, as do the bar staff, who pour perfect Guinness. Irish music helps generate Emerald Isle charm.

 D6 100 W. GRAND AVE.
312-836-0066

FUNKY BUDDHA LOUNGE

A diverse mix of club-hoppers sidle up to Buddha sculptures and each other in a series of lush Asian-inspired rooms. Sophisticated hip-hop, soul, and house tunes complete the vibe.

 D2 728 W. GRAND AVE.
312-666-1695

GOODBAR

Goodbar features three distinct environments: wood-topped bars and funky murals downstairs, a second-floor lounge with red walls and black leather couches, and a rooftop deck.

 F3 2512 N. HALSTED ST.
773-296-9700

GREEN MILL

Al Capone's Prohibition-era hideout is now a smoky, crammed bar that boasts a stellar jazz lineup, from vocalists to big band. Original Uptown Poetry Slam held Sundays.
OFF MAP 4802 N. BROADWAY ST. (AT LAWRENCE AVE.) 773-878-5552

HARRY'S VELVET ROOM

One of Chicago's archetypal lounges, subterranean Harry's sets the scene with red velvet panels, leather banquettes, and a draped chandelier. Candlelight heightens the ambience.

 D6 56 W. ILLINOIS ST.
312-527-5600

HIDEOUT

The locus of Chicago's burgeoning alt-country scene, Hideout lures sincere, denim-clad listeners by headlining regulars like Devil in a Woodpile and other Bloodshot Records artists.

 C5 1354 W. WABANSIA AVE.
773-227-4433

HOTSIE TOTSIE

This nautical bar has copper tables, anchors on the wall, and long-time patrons who spin yarns over Scotch on the rocks.

 F5 8 E. DIVISION ST.
312-337-9128

HOUSE OF BLUES

Both a clean, tightly run chain and a folksy space with outsider art, HOB hosts top-name rock, funk, and occasionally blues. Stop by for Gospel Brunch Sundays.

 E6 329 N. DEARBORN ST.
312-923-2000

JAZZ SHOWCASE

Claiming fame as the world's second-oldest jazz club, Joe Segal's Jazz Showcase has hosted sax, piano, and vocals since 1947, when Charlie "Bird" Parker reigned. No smoking.

 D6 59 W. GRAND AVE.
312-670-2473

JILLY'S / RETRO CLUB

Jilly's draws an older crowd of Sinatra fans who sip port or champagne while listening to piano jazz and crooners. Disco lives at the adjacent Retro Club.

A1 1007 N. RUSH ST.
312-664-1001

JOY-BLUE

Blue tablecloths, flickering candles, and deejay-driven sounds create a cool ambience in which brew drinkers mingle with martini sippers while shooting pool or taking in the artwork.

 A1 1401 W. IRVING PARK RD.
773-477-3330

KINGSTON MINES

Wander between two stages hosting local blues legends like Eddy Clearwater. Fuel up for boisterous late-night performances with Cajun and soul food from the kitchen.

 F3 2548 N. HALSTED ST.
773-477-4646

LE PASSAGE

Enter this glitzy subterranean bar through an alley; then share a Scorpion Bowl in the Yow Bar or hit the dance floor among the well-heeled patrons.

 A1 1 OAK PLACE
312-255-0022

LIQUID KITTY

Loud colors, psychedelic patterns, and enough leopard prints to alarm PETA make a bold contrast to the cool, deejay-spun music and laid-back patrons in basic black.

 B5 228 W. CHICAGO AVE.
312-266-6369

MAP ROOM

Travelers trek to this side-street coffeehouse-cum-tavern for the global draught beers and shelves of travel guides. Tuesday's International Night offers a free spread from a featured country.

 B2 1949 N. HOYNE AVE.
773-252-7636

METRO/SMART BAR

Joe Shanahan's pivotal rock venue has launched dozens of bands, including locals like Smashing Pumpkins. Head downstairs to Smart Bar for a post-show brew.

B2 3730 N. CLARK ST.
773-549-0203

MURPHY'S BLEACHERS

 The storied bar behind the right-field bleachers has been a hit with Cubs fans since the '30s. Its rooftop overlooks the ballpark. Expect hordes on game day.

 B3 3655 N. SHEFFIELD AVE.
773-281-5356

OLD TOWN ALE HOUSE

Soak up local character while playing pinball or reading a complimentary paperback. Old Town's mural and photos pay tribute to barflies come and gone, including John Belushi.

 D4 219 W. NORTH AVE.
312-944-7020

POPS FOR CHAMPAGNE

The celebrities at this posh jazz and champagne bar include Veuve Clicquot and Dom Perignon. Order caviar and bubbly by the fireplace or in the garden.

 D3 2934 N. SHEFFIELD AVE.
773-472-1000

RED LION

Rumor has it that this creaky English pub is haunted. A red telephone "box," proper pints of ale, and pub grub like fish-and-chips cater to Anglophiles.

 F3 2446 N. LINCOLN AVE.
773-348-2695

REDNOFIVE/FIFTH FLOOR

Join the hardcore dancers at Rednofive's smoky basement party hosted by deejays spinning fresh house beats. Fifth Floor takes a more upscale, champagne-bar approach.

 D2 440 N. HALSTED ST.
312-733-6699

SIGNATURE LOUNGE
Savor breathtaking views of the lakeshore at this romantic bar on the 96th floor of the John Hancock Center.

 B2 875 N. MICHIGAN AVE.
312-787-7230

SINIBAR
This sexy Moroccan den, filled with rugs and modified poof chairs, exudes an exotic ambience. Bask in hip-hop and soul grooves while nibbling gourmet treats.

 D2 1540 N. MILWAUKEE AVE.
773-278-7797

SLOW DOWN: LIFE'S TOO SHORT
Park your yacht and climb inside this haven of kitsch – think mounted bass, hanging lingerie, and '80s and '90s pop. The deck offers river and skyline views.

 F5 1177 N. ELSTON AVE.
773-384-1040

SOUTHPORT LANES & BILLIARDS
Live pinsetters work the four lanes in the former Schlitz bar, which also boasts pool tables in the back room. Enjoy the laid-back atmosphere with a microbrew.

 C1 3325 N. SOUTHPORT AVE.
773-472-6600

SPY BAR
Shake it beneath strobe lights on the packed dance floor or perch on a leopard-print barstool and spy the beautiful people mingling against an exposed-brick backdrop.

 C5 646 N. FRANKLIN ST.
312-587-8779

TANTRUM
Tantrum's plush interior, with its fanciful seating and polished-wood bar, offers an oasis in this nightlife-deprived part of the Loop. Sample the creative martini selection.

 E2 1023 S. STATE ST.
312-939-9160

TRADER VIC'S
The legendary creator of the Mai Tai opened this eponymous bar in the Palmer House Hilton, filling it with bamboo and Polynesian tchotchkes.

 B2 17 E. MONROE ST.
312-917-7317

WEBSTER'S WINE BAR
Choose from 40 wines by the glass in this inviting, candlelit atmosphere, which caters to connoisseurs and novices alike. Pizzas and cheese plates prime the palate.

 B4 1480 W. WEBSTER ST.
773-868-0608

WHISKEY BLUE
In the W City Center, Rande Gerber's fashionable establishment appeals to the velvet-rope crowd. Repose in leather chairs for intimate conversation while counting designer labels.

 B5 172 W. ADAMS ST.
312-782-4933

WILD HARE
Live Afro-Caribbean music and bottles of Red Stripe keep this friendly bar hopping. Look for the sign: Wild Hare and Singing Armadillo Frog Sanctuary.

 B2 3530 N. CLARK ST.
773-327-4273

WOODLAWN TAP
Honorary watering hole for the University of Chicago since late owner Jimmy Wilson opened it in 1949, the renovated Tap draws local workers and university professors.

 C3 1172 E. 55TH ST.
773-643-5516

ZEBRA LOUNGE
Housed in a vintage apartment building, this tiny lounge scintillates with zebra-striped walls and a mirrored bar. Sing along to piano tunes with the regulars.

 F5 1220 N. STATE PKWY.
312-642-5140

ZENTRA
Pass a hookah pipe filled with flavored tobacco while lounging in a fabric-draped booth, or head to the upstairs loft for dance music.

D6 923 W. WEED ST.
312-787-0400

OUTDOORS

ALTA VISTA TERRACE

 Lined with century-old rowhouses, the bizarrely beautiful 3800 block of Alta Vista Terrace is known as "the Street of 40 Doors." Each building has a twin on the other side of the street.

 A2 START AT N. ALTA VISTA TER. AND GRACE ST.

ARCHITECTURE RIVER CRUISE

See more than 50 notable sights on the Chicago Architecture Foundation's 90-minute river cruise. It's popular, so buy tickets in advance. Spring-fall.

 E2 DOCK LOCATION: SOUTHEAST CORNER OF MICHIGAN AVE. AND WACKER DR. 312-922-3432

▲

ASTOR STREET

Fashionable 19th-century homes stretch out along the 1200-1600 blocks of Astor Street. Note the historic Frank Lloyd Wright–designed Charnley House (1365 N. Astor St.).

 F5 START AT ASTOR AND DIVISION STS.

BANK ONE PLAZA / CHAGALL MOSAIC

 Brown-bag it with Loop workers enjoying the noontime concerts at this lively plaza, home of Marc Chagall's surrealist mosaic *The Four Seasons.*

 B6 DEARBORN AND MONROE STS.

BURNHAM PARK

Joggers and cyclists can go for miles along the lake on this lengthy ribbon of greenspace that starts south of Grant Park and stretches down to Promontory Point.

 A5 1559 S. LAKESHORE DR. 312-747-7009

CHICAGO ARCHITECTURE FOUNDATION TOURS

Knowledgeable docents lead guests on walking tours – or crash courses – of Chicago architecture year-round. Among the best: the two-hour roundup of Loop skyscrapers.

 C2 224 S. MICHIGAN AVE. 312-922-3432

COMISKEY PARK

For baseball fans needing a ballgame fix, catching the White Sox at their South Side home is a good alternative to tracking down elusive Cubs tickets.

OVERVIEW MAP E4 333 W. 35TH ST. 312-674-1000

FAMILY GOLF CENTER

Rent some clubs and hit the links near the lake at this nine-hole golf course that includes chipping and putting greens, as well as a year-round driving range.

 E3 221 N. COLUMBUS DR. 312-616-1234

FEDERAL CENTER / CALDER'S *FLAMINGO*

 Famed architect Ludwig Mies van der Rohe's International Style is beautifully executed in the black, steel-and-glass shell of the Dirksen Building. Alexander Calder's graceful *Flamingo* sculpture stands in the nearby plaza.

 C6 219 S. DEARBORN ST.

GRACELAND CEMETERY

 The resident list of the city's most prestigious cemetery reads like a who's who of Chicago history: Daniel Burnham, Marshall Field,

Louis Sullivan. Stop by the main office for a free map.

 A2 4001 N. CLARK ST. 773-525-1105

GRANT PARK
See SIGHTS, p. 13.

 E3 337 E. RANDOLPH ST. 312-742-7648

HISTORY OF PRINTING MURAL
 This colorful scene rendered above the entry to the Second Franklin Building depicts the early days of printing, which flourished along this stretch of historic Printer's Row.

 D6 720 S. DEARBORN ST.

HORSE-DRAWN CARRIAGE RIDE
 Generally available year-round, these rides – whether you consider them a romantic ploy or symbol of slower-paced times – offer an unhurried tour of the sights under the sun or the stars.

 B2 820 N. MICHIGAN AVE. 312-266-7878

JACKSON PARK
 Highlights of this 525-acre park – described by Clarence Darrow as "the prettiest view on earth" – include the serene Osaka Garden and stellar bird-watching on Wooded Island.

 E5 6401 S. STONY ISLAND AVE. 312-747-6187

JAMES R. THOMPSON CENTER
Chicagoans either love or hate this Helmut Jahn–designed glass-and-steel spaceship/seat of state government. Equally mind-boggling is Jean Dubuffet's black-and-white fiberglass sculpture that sits outside.

A5 100 W. RANDOLPH ST. 312-814-6684

LAKEFRONT PATH
Join the parade of in-line skaters and cyclists on this 18-mile path along the lake. You can rent all

the equipment from Bike Chicago at the North Avenue Beach boathouse.

 D6 START AT NORTH AVENUE BEACH, 1600 N. LAKE SHORE DR. 773-327-2706 (BIKE CHICAGO)

LINCOLN PARK/LINCOLN PARK ZOO
See SIGHTS, p. 17.

 B4 ZOO: 2200 N. CANNON DR. 312-742-2000

MIDWAY PLAISANCE
 This mile-long, block-wide grassy swath hosted the Colombian Exposition in 1893. It now welcomes joggers, soccer games, ice skaters, and cross-country skiers.

 E2 BTWN. 59TH AND 60TH STS., STONY ISLAND AND COTTAGE GROVE AVES.

MILLENNIUM PARK
This ambitious and controversial pet project of Mayor Daley *(fils)* boasts the coolest ice-skating rink in the city.

A2 55 N. MICHIGAN AVE. 312-742-7529

NORTHALSTED MARKET DAYS
Sexual orientation doesn't matter at this straight-friendly gay and lesbian weekend festival in August that draws drag queens and frat boys alike. It's flamboyant, fun, and wildly popular.

 B3 N. HALSTED ST. BTWN. ADDISON ST. AND BELMONT AVE. 773-868-3010

NORTH AVENUE BEACH
 A boat-shaped beach house marks this bustling, mile-long strip of sand that's packed with families, swinging singles, and beach volleyball players from Memorial Day to Labor Day.

 D6 1600 N. LAKE SHORE DR. 312-742-7529

OAK STREET BEACH
Welcome to the Midwest's version of the Riviera, where bathing Gold Coast beauties congregate on Chicago's toniest beach.

 F6 1100 N. LAKE SHORE DR. 312-752-7529

PICASSO SCULPTURE

Theories abound, but no one really knows what Picasso's sculpture in Daley Plaza is supposed to be. Some think it's a bird or a woman with flowing hair. Children seem to think it's a giant slide.

 A6 WASHINGTON BLVD. AND DEARBORN ST.

PROMONTORY POINT

Jutting into Lake Michigan, this focal point of Burnham Park is a haven for swimmers and picnickers. From here, take in views of the Chicago skyline and the shores of Indiana.

 C6 5491 SOUTH SHORE DR.

THE ROOKERY

 This Burnham and Root-designed building boasts a stunning lobby redesigned by Frank Lloyd Wright. It rests in a spot where hundreds of pigeons once roosted, hence its name.

 C5 209 S. LASALLE ST.

SOLDIER FIELD

Da Bears' Doric-columned den is getting an overhaul that is scheduled to be complete in 2003. Until then, football fans have to travel downstate to cheer on the home team.

 B4 425 E. MCFETRIDGE DR. 312-559-1212 (TICKETS)

SOUTH KENWOOD HISTORIC DISTRICT

This 23-square block area boasts some of the city's finest mansions built between 1870 and 1930. The proud owners have restored many of these Italian villas and Frank Lloyd Wright homes.

A3 BTWN. 47TH AND 51ST STS., BLACKSTONE AND DREXEL AVES.

TASTE OF CHICAGO

 Sample the city's culinary creations with the masses in sunny Grant Park during this 10-day summer ritual that runs from late June through early July.

 C3 GRANT PARK, ENTER AT JACKSON AND COLUMBUS DRS. 312-744-3370

WASHINGTON PARK

 Plenty of picnic tables, a pool, and a fishing pond make Washington Park a popular place to be on warm weekends. Baseball diamonds and cricket fields round out the amenities.

 C1 5531 S. MARTIN LUTHER KING DR. 312-747-6823

WAVELAND TENNIS COURTS

Regulars swing their racquets from Memorial Day to Labor Day at these 20 courts nestled next to famed Lake Shore Drive. Reservations taken at on-site trailer for a nominal fee.

 A4 WAVELAND AVE. AND LAKE SHORE DR. 312-742-7673

WICKER PARK

 Bohemian hipsters flip through *Utne Readers* on this triangular patch of grass, while dogs flirt in the park's fenced in corner.

 E2 1425 N. DAMEN AVE. 312-742-7553

WRIGLEY BUILDING

Each night, floodlights blast the creamy white terra-cotta façade of this chewing-gum empire headquarters in one of the country's most elaborate commercial lighting displays.

 D2 410 N. MICHIGAN AVE. 312-644-2121

WRIGLEY FIELD

See SIGHTS, p. 28.

B3 1060 W. ADDISON ST. 773-404-2827, 800-843-2827 (TICKETS)

Ⓗ **HOTELS**

CHIC HOTELS

W CHICAGO LAKESHORE
Chicago's second W has become the latest stomping ground of the jazzy jet set. Hip business travelers and in-the-know locals sip martinis in the sexy, candlelit lobby and the décor is straight up Asian simplicity with a twist of luxury. Wired rooms keep guests connected while wacky touches – like the Pez dispensers at the minibar – keep them entertained. Patrons needing odd, or oddly timed, services will enjoy the "whatever, whenever" attentiveness of the staff. $$$

 C4 644 N. LAKE SHORE DR.
312-943-9200 OR 877-946-8357

CITY SUITES HOTEL
Popular with gay and lesbian travelers, City Suites has an art deco air that's both chic and retro. Its location is perfect for hitting the far-out boutiques along Belmont Avenue. $

 C3 933 W. BELMONT AVE.
773-404-3400 OR 800-248-9108

HOTEL ALLEGRO
Starting with the Tootsie Rolls at the front desk, quirky touches abound in the hip Allegro. Social guests will enjoy the complimentary evening wine hour. $

 A5 171 W. RANDOLPH ST.
312-236-0123 OR 800-643-1500

HOTEL BURNHAM
Curtains adorned with musical references and Nintendo in every room add to the eccentric ambience of this whimsical hotel, fashioned out of the historic Reliance Building. $$

 A1 1 W. WASHINGTON BLVD.
312-782-1111 OR 877-294-9712

HOUSE OF BLUES HOTEL
This unorthodox den for people on the go is awash in vivid colors. Look for the fragrant mood crystal left on your pillow at turndown and check out Sunday's Gospel Brunch, a feast of Southern-style cooking and gospel music. $$

 E6 333 N. DEARBORN ST.
312-245-0333 OR 800-235-6397

LE MERIDIEN
An endless line of Louis Vuitton luggage rolls through the boldly colored lobby of this base for shopping weekenders. The full-service staff can even set guests up with a Nordstrom personal shopper. $$$

 D2 520 N. MICHIGAN AVE.
312-645-1500 OR 800-543-4300

THE SILVERSMITH
This architectural gem on Jewelers Row adorns its rooms in the Arts and Crafts style of the late 1890s. A free dessert bar is offered Monday through Thursday. $

 B2 10 S. WABASH AVE.
312-372-7696 OR 800-227-6963

SWISSOTEL
Run like a Swiss clock, this triangular hotel caters to management types with its executive level amenities. Guests can work out to a great view in the 42nd-floor gym. $$$

 E3 323 E. WACKER DR.
312-565-0565 OR 800-637-9477

W CHICAGO CITY CENTER
This financial industry favorite hosts business travellers in its 1940s Hollywood-style rooms, complete with the W's signature pillow-top mattresses. $$$

 B5 172 W. ADAMS ST.
312-332-1200 OR 877-946-8357

WESTIN CHICAGO RIVER NORTH
Expect service and style at this sleek property perched near the Chicago River. Complimentary shoe shines are among the amenities, and the rooms are dressed in clean lines and soothing colors. $$

 E6 320 N. DEARBORN ST.
312-744-1900 OR 800-937-8461

GRAND HOTELS

RITZ-CARLTON
The highly acclaimed Ritz-Carlton is in a league of its own. This luxurious beauty is favored by celebrities, CEOs, and others unconcerned with disposable income. The grand lobby, four-star restaurant, and sweeping views would stand out at any other hotel, but here, the superlative service is the signature dish. The seasoned staff is happy to deliver shoelaces, saline, and a hundred other necessities atop a silver tray at any time of day. $$$

 B2 160 E. PEARSON ST.
312-266-1000 OR 800-621-6906

CHICAGO HILTON AND TOWERS
This gargantuan hotel is a favorite among conventioneers and Hollywood location scouts – it's been used for numerous films, including *The Fugitive*. Exercise buffs will appreciate the sprawling athletic club. $$

 D2 720 S. MICHIGAN AVE.
312-922-4400 OR 800-445-8667

DRAKE HOTEL
This grande dame still looks smashing even though she's in her 80s. A venerable Chicago icon, the Drake embodies class, right down to the upholstered elevator seats and the harpist who plays during high tea. $$$

 A2 140 E. WALTON PLACE
312-787-2200 OR 800-553-7253

FOUR SEASONS
Featuring gorgeous surroundings and an award-winning spa, this luxurious property offers almost every amenity you can imagine. The concierge might even be able to snag Oprah tickets for guests. $$$

 B2 120 E. DELAWARE PLACE
312-280-8800 OR 800-332-3442

HYATT REGENCY MCCORMICK PLACE
If you're going to a McCormick Place convention, there's nothing more convenient: an enclosed walkway links both buildings. To unwind, rent a hotel bike for a spin on the lakefront path nearby. $$

 E4 2233 S. MARTIN LUTHER KING DR.
312-567-1234 OR 800-233-1234

OLD TOWN CHICAGO BED & BREAKFAST INN
This art deco mansion is sumptuously outfitted with 13-inch-thick mattresses, a rooftop deck, and a spacious drawing room complete with marble fireplace and Baldwin grand piano. Guests can book a room or the entire house. $

 E3 1442 N. NORTH PARK AVE.
312-440-9268

OMNI AMBASSADOR EAST
A favorite of Frank Sinatra and the Rat Pack, this historic landmark boasts unobtrusive service and a discreet location that still attracts the occasional celebrity. The stunning lobby features Italian marble and crystal chandeliers. $

 E5 1301 N. STATE PKWY.
312-787-7200 OR 800-843-6664

PALMER HOUSE HILTON
Conventioneers take up many of the 1,600-plus rooms in this historic, palatial property. The French salon-style painting on the lobby ceiling, with its 33 individual oil compositions, is phenomenal. $$

 B2 17 E. MONROE ST.
312-726-7500 OR 800-774-1500

RENAISSANCE CHICAGO HOTEL
Close to the Loop and Mag Mile, this lavish property will appeal to those with a corporate expense account. On the premises, a Kinko's perfect for procrastinators. $$

 E6 1 W. WACKER DR.
312-372-7200 OR 800-468-3571

QUAINT HOTELS

WHEELER MANSION

Guests with an eye for detail will have plenty to look at in this 11-room Italianate mansion filled with European antiques and oil paintings. This historic home predates the Chicago fire and it's hard to tell the original from the recreated. Beds donning 360-count, double-twisted linens and gourmet breakfasts served on bone china are among Wheeler Mansion's pampering amenities. $$

 D4 2020 S. CALUMET AVE.
312-945-2020

CONGRESS PLAZA HOTEL

Once favored by presidents, the historic Congress Plaza Hotel has seen better days. But the stellar location near Grant Park and affordable price keep customers coming. $

 D2 520 S. MICHIGAN AVE.
312-427-3800 OR 800-635-1666

FLEMISH HOUSE

Private kitchens and baths make this meticulously restored 1890s graystone rowhouse ideal for extended stays along the Gold Coast. Some rooms have fireplaces. $

 F5 68 E. CEDAR ST.
312-664-9981

GOLD COAST GUEST HOUSE

In addition to the pleasant rooms at this brick townhouse, guests can get the lowdown on Chicago from the friendly owner over a glass of wine in the garden. $

 F4 113 W. ELM ST.
312-337-0361

HOUSE OF TWO URNS B&B

Kitchy knickknacks and antique cameras are scattered throughout this delightfully eccentric bed-and-breakfast. The spacious upstairs suite is perfect for families. $

 E4 1239 N. GREENVIEW AVE.
773-235-1408

HYATT ON PRINTERS ROW

While it may not have a full suite of deluxe amenities, this hotel can boast attentive service, well-equipped rooms, and a convenient Loop location. $$

 D6 500 S. DEARBORN ST.
312-986-1234 OR 800-233-1234

THE SENECA

This bargain property lets guests stay in the heart of Mag Mile, but maintains an air of seclusion. Most rooms include tiny kitchens. $

 B2 200 E. CHESTNUT ST.
312-787-8900 OR 800-800-6261

THE TREMONT

This worn-around-the-edges resting spot enjoys a prime location only a block away from Mag Mile. The smallish green-and-yellow rooms are filled with Colonial-style furniture. $

 B2 100 E. CHESTNUT ST.
312-751-1900 OR 800-621-8133

WHITEHALL HOTEL

Striped dust ruffles and Chippendale desks give this 221-room luxury hotel an old English flavor. All rooms provide guests with terry robes and the suites offer city views. $$

 B2 105 E. DELAWARE PLACE
312-944-6300 OR 800-948-4255

WICKER PARK INN

This may be a 115-year-old home, but there's no trace of frilly curtains in the cheerfully colored, mod-quaint rooms. The owners will happily pick up guests arriving on the El. $

 E3 1329 N. WICKER PARK AVE.
773-486-2743

WOODED ISLE SUITES

Parents and professors visiting near-by University of Chicago find spartan, yet cozy, digs at this small vintage property. $

 D4 5750 S. STONY ISLAND AVE.
773-288-5578

ROMANTIC HOTELS

PENINSULA
Mood lighting at the touch of a button, in-room massages, baths with flower petals – the Peninsula lavishes guests with romance despite its reputation as a first-rate business hotel. Nightstand panels control almost every aspect of the elegant rooms, leaving you little reason to get out of bed except for a trip to the relaxing spa or a splash in the deep-soak tub. **$$$**

 C2 108 E. SUPERIOR ST.
312-337-2888 OR 866-288-8889

FAIRMONT
Close to Grant Park, this urban oasis offers elegant, spacious rooms and courteous service. The oversized tubs can be filled with sensual oils for a blissful bathing experience. **$$$**

 E3 200 N. COLUMBUS DR.
312-565-8000 OR 800-526-2008

HOTEL INTER-CONTINENTAL
Service can be snooty at this art deco masterpiece, but the luxurious indoor pool is unparalleled. Down pillows and plush robes surround guests with comfort. **$$**

 D2 505 N. MICHIGAN AVE.
312-944-4100 OR 800-327-0200

HOTEL MONACO
Along with the standard free shoe shines and morning newspapers, this high-end boutique throws in a pet goldfish upon request to keep during your stay. Special rooms have extra-long beds for taller travelers. **$$**

 E1 225 N. WABASH AVE.
312-960-8503 OR 866-610-0081

MAJESTIC HOTEL
The Majestic's quiet location, English country estate atmosphere, and crackling lobby fireplace make it a relaxing retreat. Guests who want to stay in can order room service from several nearby restaurants. **$**

 B4 528 W. BROMPTON AVE.
773-404-3499 OR 800-727-5108

MILLENNIUM KNICKERBOCKER
The former Playboy Towers now caters to a more straight-laced crowd. Guests linger at the martini bar in the softly lit lobby before retiring to their canopied beds. **$$**

 A2 163 E. WALTON PLACE
312-751-8100 OR 800-621-8140

SUTTON PLACE HOTEL
Doormen welcome guests by name to this art deco-inspired haven that prides itself on personalized service, such as free lifts to the Loop. Enjoy deep-soaking tubs, down duvets, and soundproof rooms. **$$$**

 A1 21 E. BELLEVUE PLACE
312-266-2100 OR 800-606-8188

TALBOTT HOTEL
The 149-room Talbott has the personality of a boutique, but the amenities of a big hotel. An English theme pervades the lobby, and the bar attracts a refined crowd. **$**

 A1 20 E. DELAWARE PLACE
312-944-4970 OR 800-825-2688

WILLOWS HOTEL
The Willows, with its rustic French atmosphere and quiet location, is a tranquil retreat. If you must work, the spacious desks and data ports in every room accommodate. **$**

 E4 555 W. SURF ST.
773-528-8400 OR 800-787-3108

WINDY CITY B&B INN
This peaceful Victorian mansion offers a quiet location and an ivy-covered garden perfect for lounging on warm days. For ultimate privacy, book a self-contained apartment in the cozy coach house. **$**

 F4 607 W. DEMING PLACE
773-248-7091 OR 877-897-7091

CITY ESSENTIALS

AIRPORTS

Chicago's O'Hare International Airport (800-832-6352) has reclaimed its status as the world's busiest airport. Located 17 miles northwest of the city, the airport sees more than 190,000 travelers pass through daily. Passengers arriving at O'Hare's domestic terminals can board regional buses at the Bus Shuttle Center, which is located on the first floor of the main parking facility. The 24-hour Chicago Transit Authority (CTA) Blue line is located near Terminal 2 on the lower level. If you arrive at the international terminal, take the free, 24-hour Airport Transit System to the main terminals to catch a bus or train. The Blue line takes approximately 45 minutes to get to the city, while a drive takes anywhere from 30 minutes to significantly more than an hour during heavy traffic.

Located 10 miles southwest of downtown, Midway Airport (773-838-0600) is becoming a popular alternative for domestic and limited international flights. Regional buses are located on the lower level roadway at doors 2LL and 3LL. The CTA Orange line also has a stop on the lower level at the east end of the terminal. Trains run between 3:55 A.M. and 12:51 A.M. nightly, at least every 15 minutes. The ride into downtown takes about 20-30 minutes. Vehicle pick-up services and an information booth are located in the main lobby at the airport's central entrance. A taxi or car ride into downtown from Midway takes 20-50 minutes.

The Continental Airport Express (312-454-7800) offers a daily connection between O'Hare or Midway and the city or northern suburbs between 6 A.M. and 11:30 P.M. The cost is approximately $20 from O'Hare, $15 from Midway. Advance reservations are recommended. The Omega Airport Shuttle (773-483-6634), which operates 6:45 A.M.–11:45 P.M. at O'Hare and 7 A.M.–10 P.M. at Midway, offers service between the two airports. A one-way fare costs $20.

Approximate cab fares into downtown are $40 from O'Hare and $25 from Midway.

PUBLIC TRANSPORTATION

The Chicago Transit Authority (CTA) runs quite smoothly throughout the city with a system of buses, subway, and elevated (El) trains.

CTA train lines are color-coded (Red, Blue, Brown, Green, Orange, Purple, and Yellow) and designated by beginning and end points (for example, the Red line also is the Howard-95-Dan Ryan line), with the final destination displayed prominently on the front and sides of the train. Pay attention to trains becoming express with little warning – they often skip numerous stops and head directly to the next major stop. Trains run every 3-12 minutes during weekday rush hours and 6-20 minutes at other times. The Blue (Forest Park-O'Hare Airport) and Red lines run 24 hours, seven days a week. Between 1:30 and 4:30 A.M., the Red line runs every 15 minutes, the Blue line once an hour.

CTA rides cost $1.50 each way and $.30 for a transfer (two additional rides within two hours). Use exact fare in coins or, preferably, buy a rechargeable Transit Card. Transit Cards and Visitor Passes may be found in most El stations or at currency exchanges and Jewel and Dominick's grocery stores. Call 888-968-7282 for further information.

In general, buses follow one street for the entire route, so it's often necessary to switch to another bus to reach your destination. Buses run every 5-10 minutes during rush hour, 8-20 minutes during normal day and evening hours, and Night Owl routes (labeled "24 hours" on the bus charts) run roughly every 30 minutes. Note the destination posted in the bus's front window to determine direction of travel. Board with exact fare of $1.50 or a Transit Card.

Architecturally significant Union Station (210 S. Canal St., 800-872-7245) is the city's main train terminal, with about 50 Amtrak trains servicing Chicago every day. Metra (312-322-6777) trains travel throughout northeast Illinois, stopping at four downtown terminals: LaSalle Street, Randolph Street, Ogilvie Transportation Center, and Union Station.

TAXIS
Taxis are plentiful in most areas of Chicago. In rare instances you may have to call ahead — on a busy holiday or late at night in less-traveled areas — but in most cases you will find a taxi quickly by simply hailing one. If the light on top of the cab is on, it is available. Taxis charge $1.90 upon entrance and $.50 for each additional passenger. From that point, it costs $1.60 per mile or $2 for every six minutes of waiting time.

The shared ride program allows up to four passengers not traveling together to ride together from the airports or McCormick Place convention center for a discounted rate. The cost per person is $19 from O'Hare, $14 from Midway, and $5 from McCormick Place to destinations within designated boundaries.

CHECKER TAXI: 312-243-2537
FLASH CAB CO.: 773-561-4444
YELLOW CAB: 312-829-4222

DRIVING AND RENTING A CAR
Chicago's driving conditions are notorious, especially along the tollways and Lake Shore Drive where cars and cabs reach perilous speeds

(except during rush hour, when traffic often comes to a standstill). If you plan to leave the city during your visit, multiple rental companies have branches throughout the city, especially in the Loop and at both airports:

AVIS: 800-331-1212
DOLLAR RENT A CAR: 773-686-2030
ENTERPRISE RENT-A-CAR: 312-565-6518

There are large, multi-story parking lots in the Loop and smaller lots outside downtown. Metered spots are difficult to find, expensive, and usually have a very short time limit. Some densely populated neighborhoods, such as Lincoln Park and Lake View, regulate parking on side streets to permit-holding residents only. Don't assume they won't catch you — police cruise these streets frequently.

WEATHER
Chicago experiences four distinct seasons with extreme variations in temperature. In general, summers are warm and humid, winters are snowy and cold, and spring and autumn have some of the best weather with warm, clear days and crisp evenings. Lake Michigan has a regulating effect, giving off temperate air masses that reduce oppressive summer temperatures and take the edge off bitter winter chills.

Average low temperatures in January and February are in the mid- to upper teens, with average highs in the upper 20s and average snowfall around nine inches. Temperatures increase during April and May to average highs of around 65, with July and August reaching the mid-80s and about four inches of rainfall. By the end of October, lows may again reach freezing but daytime temperatures are pleasant, in the low to mid-60s.

No matter what season your visit, Chicago's weather can change on a dime. Temperatures can rise or fall dramatically during a single day – even as much as 30 degrees – so dress for variable conditions.

HOURS

Chicago is second to none in terms of nightlife. Wild dance clubs, smoky blues joints, and swank lounges cater to the city's night owls. A growing number of establishments stay open until 4 or 5 A.M. on weekends. Most restaurants close at 11 P.M. or midnight, but some stay open until 2 A.M. or later on weekends. For those who need sustenance after bar-hopping or clubbing, there is no dearth of 24-hour diners and late-night lounges serving gourmet nibbles.

DISABLED ACCESS

The city provides special services for handicapped visitors, offering disabled access to major destinations and sign-language interpretation at many museums and theaters. Numerous CTA stations are accessible by wheelchair. CTA maps, found at most El stations, indicate which stations have elevators. Also, 112 of 140 bus routes are fully accessible, with lifts and ramps made available upon request.

SAFETY

As Chicago is a large urban city, use common sense when traveling. Be aware of your belongings at all times, especially in crowds and on public transportation. Late at night, unless traveling in a large group, you may want to take a taxi back to your hotel instead of navigating public transportation. Do not enter empty El cars alone at any time.

A good general rule is to avoid empty streets and stay in busy, well-lighted areas after dark. If you feel threatened, leave the area immediately. Areas south (South Loop and beyond) and west (beyond West Loop, River West, and Bucktown/Wicker Park) of downtown can be unsafe after dark, so visit during the day instead or travel directly to your destination via taxi. In fact, areas of

the Loop are nearly deserted late at night, except in the theater district. When visiting Hyde Park, you may feel more comfortable opting for the CTA No. 6 Jeffery Express bus instead of the Green or Red lines – a must after dark.

HEALTH AND EMERGENCY SERVICES

The following hospitals run 24-hour emergency rooms:

ADVOCATE ILLINOIS MASONIC MEDICAL CENTER

 D3 838 W. WELLINGTON AVE. 773-296-7078

NORTHWESTERN MEMORIAL HOSPITAL

 C3 240 E. ERIE ST. 312-926-5188

SAINT JOSEPH HOSPITAL

 E5 2900 N. LAKE SHORE DR. 773-665-3086

UNIVERSITY OF CHICAGO HOSPITAL

D2 901 E. 58TH ST. 773-702-6250

In emergency, dial 911 for police and ambulance service. For non-emergencies, 311 reaches the police. The fire department number is 312-347-1313.

PHARMACIES

CVS PHARMACY

 D6 1714 N. SHEFFIELD AVE. 312-640-5160

OSCO DRUG

 F4 1165 N. CLARK ST. 312-280-8371

WALGREENS

 B2 25 S. WABASH AVE. 312-641-1856

 B2 757 N. MICHIGAN AVE. 312-664-4000

MEDIA AND COMMUNICATIONS

Main area codes in Chicago are 312 (downtown) and 773 (north, south, and west city). Suburban prefixes are 708, 847, and 630.

It seems everyone in Chicago has a mobile phone. There are few regulations regarding their use, though common courtesy dictates that people should switch off phones in certain public spaces such as theaters, restaurants, and spas. Except for taxi drivers, people behind the wheel are allowed to talk on the phone while driving, but this practice is not advised. To rent a phone, try RentCell (800-404-3093).

Public telephones are still found in most public buildings and CTA stations. They are coin operated, though you may find it easier to buy a phone card with a designated personal identification number. Walgreens and Osco Drug both offer phone cards in many denominations, and you can add value by phone using a credit card.

The Chicago Public Library (312-747-4300) provides free Internet access at each of its 78 locations. For a high-tech business center, Chicago has surprisingly few Internet cafés.

AFTER-WORDS
After-Words is a bookstore offering Internet access. Cost is $2.50 for 15 minutes, or purchase a five-hour block for $20.

 D1 23 E. ILLINOIS ST.
312-464-1110

OFF THE WALL WIRELESS CAFE
The cafe has DSL Internet service for $9 per hour or 15 cents per minute.

 D2 1904 W. NORTH AVE.
773-782-0000

The central post office is the Fort Dearborn branch at 540 N. Dearborn St. (312-644-0485). Hours are weekdays 7:30 A.M.–5 P.M. and Saturday 7:30 A.M.–1 P.M.

The two main daily newspapers are the *Chicago Sun-Times* and the *Chicago Tribune*. Free alternative papers include the *Chicago Reader, NewCity,* and the gay and lesbian-oriented *Chicago Free Press.*

Find general city information and maps at the Chicago Office of Tourism at the Chicago Cultural Center (78 E. Washington St.) and at the Chicago Water Works (163 E. Pearson St.). The toll-free hotline of the Office of Tourism is 877-244-2246.

SMOKING
Although Chicago has restricted smoking in many offices and public buildings, its smoking policies are generally lax. Although smokers can't puff away anywhere they please, they can light up in most restaurants and nearly every bar and club in the city. Most restaurants have nonsmoking sections, but whether they are smoke-free is determined by the building's ventilation system. Cigars and pipes, however, are not allowed in many establishments. The CTA does not allow smoking anywhere on its platforms.

TIPPING
Restaurant staff and taxi drivers should be tipped between 15 and 20 percent of the total. Superior service may be rewarded with larger tips (for example, when a taxi driver helps load or unload bags). Bartenders should be paid about 15 percent of the cost of each round of drinks. Porters should be paid $1 or $2 per bag, the same per day for hotel maids.

DRY CLEANERS
BARRY'S CLEANERS

 D3 3054 N. SHEFFIELD AVE.
773-935-7696

OK CLEANERS & TAILOR

 D6 703 S. DEARBORN ST.
312-939-2973

100 W. CHESTNUT CLEANERS

 B6 100 W. CHESTNUT ST.
312-664-0587

WELLS CLEANERS

D4 1649 N. WELLS ST.
312-440-1765

STREET INDEX

MOON METRO: CHICAGO
1ST EDITION

Published by
Avalon Travel Publishing
1400 65th Street, Suite 250
Emeryville, CA 94608, USA

Distributed by Publishers Group West

Text and maps © 2002 by Avalon Travel Publishing, Inc.
All rights reserved.

CTA map © Chicago Transit Authority. Used with permission.

ISBN: 1-56691-479-5
ISSN: 1540-4951

Editor: Grace Fujimoto
Series Managers: Helen Sillett, Grace Fujimoto
Copy Editor: Kim Marks
Design: Michele Harding
Production Coordinator: Alvaro Villanueva
Graphics Coordinator: Laura VanderPloeg
Cartographers: Mike Morgenfeld, Suzanne Service
Map Editor: Naomi Adler Dancis
Typesetter: pdbd
Indexer: Olivia Solís
Contributing Writers: Jill Harrington (Museums and Galleries), Joshua Klein
(Introduction to Chicago, Neighborhoods, Sights), Heidi Moore (Shops,
Performing Arts, City Essentials), Lorilyn Rackl (Restaurants, Outdoors, Hotels)

Front cover photos: Sunset, North Avenue Beach Pier; Historic Water Tower
© Richard Cummins

Printed in China through Colorcraft Ltd., Hong Kong

Printing History
1st edition – November 2002

5 4 3 2 1

Please send all comments, corrections, additions, amendments, and critiques to:
Moon Metro: Chicago
Avalon Travel Publishing
1400 65th Street, Suite 250
Emeryville, CA 94608, USA
email: atpfeedback@avalonpub.com
website: www.moon.com

PHOTO CREDITS

35 Gourmand; page 36 Italian Village; page 36 Le Petit Folie; page 37 Maggiano's Fine Food; page 39 Penny's Noodle Shop; page 39 Pick Me Up Café; page 39 Rock n Roll McDonald's; page 40 Russian tea dolls; page 40 Shanghai Terrace; page 40 Soul Kitchen; page 40 Spiaggia; page 41 Trattoria no 10; page 42 Uncommon Ground; page 44 Crow's Nest; page 44 Spice House; page 44 Ultimo; page 44 Flashy Trash; page 44 Marshall Fields; page 44 P. 45; page 45 Quimby's; page 46 American Girl; page 46 Barbara's Bookstore; page 47 Carson P Scott metalwork; page 47 Chiasso; page 47 City Soles; page 47 chicago flat sammies; page 47 chicago pizza; page 47 Crow's Nest; page 48 Dr. Wax; page 48 Flashy Trash; page 50 Kiva; page 51 Marshall Fields; page 51 P. 45; page 52 Prarie Avenue Books; page 52 Quimby's; page 53 Spice House; page 54 Tragically Hip; page 54 Ultimo; page 56 Adler Planetarium; page 56 Betty Rymer Gallery; page 57 Chicago Historical Society; page 57 Clark House; page 57 Glessner House; page 58 Museum of Surgical Science; page 59 Spertus Jewish Museum; page 59 Terra Museum; page 60 Auditorium Theater; twin anchors; page 60 Blues Heaven Garden; page 60 Cadillac Theater; page 60 Symphony Center; page 61 Gene Siskel Film Center; page 61 Goodman Theater; page 62 Joffrey Ballet; page 62 Lyric Opera House; page 62 Music Box; page 63 Second City; page 63 Shubert Theater; page 64 Coq D'Or; page 65 Double Door; page 66 Liquid Kitty; page 66 Murphy's Bleachers; page 66 Red Lion; page 68 Alta Vista Terrace; page 68 Astor Street; page 68 Calder ©2002 Estate of Alexander Calder/Artists Rights Society (ARS), New York; page 68 Four Seasons by Chagall; page 68 Graceland Cemetary Celtic Cross; page 69 History of Printing Mural; page 69 carriage ride; page 69 Jackson Park; page 69 lakefront path; page 69 Midway Plaisance; page 69 North Avenue Beach; page 70 The Rookery; page 70 Washington Park; page 70 Wicker Park Fountain; page 72 W Hotel; page 72 W Hotel couch; page 73 Ritz-Carlton bed; page 73 Ritz-Carlton couch; page 74 Wheeler Mansion steps; page 74 Wheeler Mansion bed; page 75 Peninsula Hotel bed; page 75 Peninsula Hotel.

Other photos: cover sunset, North Avenue Beach Pier ©Richard Cummins; cover Historic Water Tower ©Richard Cummins; map 1 inner spread Savvy Traveller courtesy of Savvy Traveller; map 1 outer flap Field Museum Sue ©1999 Field Museum photo by John Weinstein; map 3 inner spread Sutton Place courtesy of The Sutton Place Hotel; map 3 inner spread Hammacher Schlemmer ©Sabrina Balthazar, courtesy of Hammacher Schlemmer; map 4 inner spread Harry Caray's courtesy of Harry Caray's Restaurant; map 4 inner spread Quincy Grill courtesy of Quincy Grille on the River; map 4 inner spread Tizi Mellou © Douglas Fogelson; map 6 inner spread Mod © Douglas Fogelson; map 7 outerflap Wrigley Field City of Chicago/©Peter J. Schulz; map 7 inner spread North Pond Restaurant courtesy of North Pond/Park Restaurants, LLC; map 7 inner spread Webster Wine Bar Matthew Grasse; map 9 inner spread Museum of Science & Industry ©Joe Ziolkowski, courtesy of Museum of Science & Insdustry; map 9 inner spread Robie House ©Hedrich Blessing, courtesy of Frank Lloyd Wright Preservation Trust; page 5 CBOT trading floor with the permission of Chicago Board of Trade, the information contained in this publication represents the views and opinions of Avalon Travel Publishing and is not necessarily the views of the Chicago Board of Trade. The Chicago Board of Trade does not guarantee nor is it responsible for the accuracy or completeness of any information presented in this publication.; page 6 Chicago Cultural Center FOLIO/©Richard Cummins; page 11 Field Museum ©The Field Museum Photo: John Weinstein; page 12 Grant Park Fountain Grant Park Fountain - FOLIO/©Richard Cummins; page 19 Museum of Science & Industry ©Joe Ziolkowski, courtesy of Museum of Science & Insdustry; page 30 North Pond courtesy of North Pond/Park Restaurants, LLC; page 27 Water Tower FOLIO/©James Lemass; page 30 Tizi Mellou © Douglas Fogelson; page 30

MOON METRO

AMSTERDAM

CHICAGO

LONDON

LOS ANGELES

NEW YORK CITY

PARIS

SAN FRANCISCO

WASHINGTON D.C.

**AVAILABLE AT YOUR FAVORITE
BOOK AND TRAVEL STORES**

UNFOLD THE CITY

MOON METRO
NEW YORK CITY

MOON METRO
PARIS

MOON METRO
SAN FRANCISCO

www.moon.com

PURPLE LINE
continues downtown
weekday rush hours

Linde
Cent
Noy
Fo
Da
D

○ Skokie 🅿️♿

YELLOW LINE
weekdays
only

BROWN LINE

RED LINE

○ O'Hare ♿
Rosemont 🅿️♿
Cumberland 🅿️♿
Harlem ♿

BLUE LINE

Kimball 🅿️♿
Kedzie 🅿️
Francisco
Rockwell
Western ♿
Damen

♿ Jefferson Park

Montrose
Irving Park
Addison

Montrose
Irving Park
Addison

Paulina
Southport

Belmont

Welline
Dive

♿ Logan
Square

California

Armit

♿ Western

Damen

Division

Chicago

Grand

Harlem ♿
Oak Park
Ridgeland
Austin
Central ♿
Laramie ♿
Cicero ♿

Pulaski♿
Conservatory-
Central Pk. Dr.
Kedzie

♿ Ashland

GREEN LINE

♿

Forest
Park ♿
Harlem
Oak
Park
Austin

Cicero

Pulaski

Kedzie-
Homan ♿

California

Western

Medical
Center ♿

♿

BLUE LINE (Forest Park Branch)

♿ Polk

♿ 18th

Racine

BLUE LINE
(Cermak
Branch)
weekdays
only

54/Cermak
Cicero ♿
Kildare
Pulaski
Central Park
Kedzie
California
Western
Hoyne

ORANGE LIN

A.

35/Arche
🅿️♿

🅿️♿Kedzie

Pulaski
🅿️♿

Western 🅿️♿

✈ Midway 🅿️♿

GREEN LIN
(Ashland
Branch)

NORTH

🅣 Free connection
between routes

♿ Accessible station

🅿️ Park 'n' Ride Lot

cta
take it.